THE GOSPEL

Illustrated by Gustav Rehberger

STORY OF JESUS

By J. Benjamin Bedenbaugh

and Gustav K. Wiencke

LUTHERAN CHURCH PRESS   PHILADELPHIA

LCA SUNDAY CHURCH SCHOOL SERIES

*This pupil's Reader is accompanied by two
"Bible Notebooks" and by a Teacher's Guide. This
material has been prepared for use in Terms
1 and 2 in the Sunday church school (7-1-2).*

9882A64   LB155

ABOUT THIS BOOK

IF YOU TAKE a flashlight with you out under the blazing stars of the night sky, its light may seem very tiny at first. As you point the flashlight upward, tiny specks of dust and moisture reflect the light and make a white beam that seems to reach far up into the dark—far enough to direct the eye to any particular part of the sky. You can use the flashlight to point out to a friend some favorite constellation or a mysterious dark spot in the Milky Way.

This book is like that flashlight. It points to the gospel story of Jesus. That story was written in different ways in the four Gospels—Matthew, Mark, Luke, and John. These four books of the Bible are witnesses to the GOOD NEWS in Jesus Christ. Nothing else can take their place. In the Gospels you can find the crisp, ancient details of deeds and sayings of Jesus as the first Christians remembered and treasured them. This book is not a substitute for the gospel story. It is a pointer to help you read the Bible yourself. Like a pointer, it can help you in your own study and enjoyment of the Gospels. In many of the short sections of this book you will find Bible references listed. In the passages listed you can find the original story as told and witnessed to in the Gospels.

What's more, you will find that the Gospels are pointers, too. They are pointers to Jesus Christ in whom God acted for our salvation in a marvelous way.

CONTENTS

I. Family Album   11
1. Why There Are Four Gospels   2. How Each Gospel Is Different   3. "Family Album" According to Luke   4. The Census and the "Sign" in Bethlehem   5. "Family Album" According to Matthew   6. How Jesus Became a Carpenter

II. Prelude to Public Ministry   31
7. How Palestine Became a Roman Province   8. Who the Sadducees and Pharisees Were   9. A Revolution Ready to Explode   10. Excitement in the Desert   11. The Greatest Enemy of Jesus   12. The Best Friends of Jesus

III. Jesus in the Public Eye   51
13. When Jesus' Neighbors Tried to Kill Him   14. People in Whom Devils Lived   15. People with a Dread Disease   16. Unexpected Faith   17. Unexpected Forgiveness   18. The Sabbath Trap   19. Jesus' Most Popular Miracle   20. The Greatest Miracle

IV. Jesus and His Disciples   78
21. A Teacher Who Was Never Dull   22. The Happy People of the Kingdom   23. Radical Righteousness   24. How Kingdom People Pray   25. Two Gates . . . Two Trees . . . Two Builders

V.   Parables of the Kingdom   99
26. He Said to Them, "Listen!"   27. The Sower
28. Buried Treasure   29. Who Is My Neighbor?
30. The Free-Spending Brother   31. Two Who
Prayed   32. The Secrets of the Kingdom of Heaven

VI.   Growing Opposition   117
33. A Dreadful Certainty   34. A Friend Who
Doubted   35. The Fate of a Prophet   36. How
They Tried to Discredit Jesus   37. What Stunned
the Temple Police   38. Cities That Had Their Last
Chance   39. What It Means to Have Faith   40.
Mystery of the Transfiguration   41. The Bitter
Cup

VII.   Journey to Jerusalem   145
42. Galilee to Bethany   43. Blind Bartimaeus and
Rich Zacchaeus   44. Incredible Miracle at Bethany

VIII.   Parting from the Disciples   157
45. Only in Jerusalem   46. Why Jesus Chose a
Donkey   47. What a Prophet Would Do in the
Temple   48. The Herodians Spring a Trap   49.
A Joke for the Sadducees   50. Parables of the
Sudden Hour   51. Everything She Had   52.
Judas, the Betrayer   53. Bread and Wine of the
"New Covenant"

IX. From Gethsemane to Golgotha   **189**

54. The Last Twenty Hours   55. Under the Olive Trees   56. Why Caiaphas Hunted for a Crime Against Religion   57. Pilate's Feud with the Jews 58. What Made Pilate Squirm   59. Ugly Death on a Dump Heap   60. What Did He Say?

X. Resurrection and Ascension   **211**

61. From an Earthly Man to a Heavenly Lord   62. Strange Tale of the Women   63. Great News from Emmaus   64. Doubt and Assurance in the Upper Room   65. A Catch of Exactly 153 Fish   66. "Ascended into Heaven"

I

FAMILY ALBUM

1. Why There Are Four Gospels

THE ANCIENT CITY of Rome lay hushed under the hot noonday sun. The streets were empty. Shops were closed. Inside the heavy brick walls of a Roman house it was cool. A man entered the front room and opened a small wooden chest. His friends had invited him to come and use the chest himself. The man was clean-shaven like a Roman aristocrat and his hair was cropped trim and short. He wore a soft white toga with such grace that its folds never seemed crumpled or disarranged.

The man looked at a rack inside the chest. It held a dozen papyrus rolls. He pulled out the largest one, then shook his head. On its outside was written in black ink "*Paulos* to the Romans." He put it back and pulled out another of the larger rolls. This was the right one. It was labeled "According to *Markon.*" Another hand had added the Greek word *euangelion* (the evangel or the gospel). Deftly he unrolled the cream-colored papyrus with his right hand and rolled up the loose end with his left, letting the neat, narrow columns of black writing pass before his eyes. When he came near the torn, broken edges at the end of the roll, he paused. His eyes scanned the columns of writing until he came to the word CENTURION. It was true! In the quiet afternoon he carefully read the crowded lines of Greek letters. If printed in English those letters would look like this:

WHENTHECENTURIONWHOSTOODFACINGHIMSAWTHAT
HETHUSBREATHEDHISLASTHESAID . . .

A Roman centurion—an officer in the army—had been there, just as his Christian friends had told him. That same centurion had been impressed by that strange man's death on a cross near Jerusalem. The man in the toga looked into the distance as he rerolled the scroll. He whispered a question to himself, "A son of God or the Son of God?" Then he slipped the large scroll back into its place in the chest.

Two thousand years ago, in the time of the Roman Caesars, this question was hotly argued. Could it be true that the man Jesus, killed as a criminal on a cross, nailed there in his nakedness, really was the Son of God? This was what the Christians claimed. Their eyes shone with a quiet joy when they said, "Jesus is the Christ of God." But why, if this were so, was he crucified? Why did he not call down a legion of heavenly warriors to proclaim his power and truth?

The man in the white toga turned back to the chest. Again he drew out the scroll. This time he started, slowly and carefully, to read the story from the beginning.

THEBEGINNINGOFTHEGOSPELOFJESUSCHRISTTHESON
OFGOD

The scroll the man held in his hand in Rome that day long ago would be valued at millions of dollars today if it still existed. It was one of the books of the first Christians who lived in Rome toward the end of the first century. It was stored in a cabinet in much the same way as the holy books of the Law and the Prophets were stored in a Jewish synagogue. That cabinet is gone. The rolls have long since disappeared. But that Gospel was copied many times. Today ancient copies of the *Gospel According to Mark* are stored in the steel vaults of great museums and universities.

It was not long until Christian writings were copied in books with pages. A book was much handier to use than a roll of parchment twenty-seven feet long. The size of a book was not limited to the length of a strip which could easily be rolled and unrolled. Several rolls could be copied into one book with many pages.

In the city of Ephesus, Christians of ancient times owned another Gospel. It was called *According to John*. In time there were dozens of different books, all of which claimed to be gospels. There was a *Gospel of Thomas,* for example, and a *Gospel of Peter*. As the years passed by, four Gospels survived and parts of them were read aloud in church every Lord's Day. They are the Gospels which we know today as Matthew, Mark, Luke, and John.

Each of these four is a book of GOOD NEWS. That is what the Greek word *euangelion* means. From this word come the words "evangel" and "evangelical." The old English word for GOOD NEWS was *good-spel*. From that we have the modern word "gospel." Long years ago when that Roman aristocrat read the scroll of Mark, he was reading a book of good news. He wanted to find out who Jesus was. He wanted especially to know why Jesus was put to death on a cross. He wanted to know just what the GOOD NEWS of the Christians was.

What was in that Gospel? Imagine that scroll unrolled on the floor of a hall—all twenty-seven feet of it. The last nine feet, or about one-third, would have been filled with the story of the last week of Jesus' life—a straightforward account of what happened to bring Jesus to the cross. The remaining eighteen feet would be filled with stories of Jesus' deeds and some of his remembered sayings. It is estimated that those eighteen feet of Gospel scroll

told of approximately thirty days between Jesus' birth and his ascension. The Gospels are not really biographies of Jesus. In ancient times no one thought of writing a person's life story the way it is done today. Writers usually did not even describe a person's appearance, nor did they tell other interesting personal things as writers usually do today.

When the writer of the Gospel of John came to the end of his scroll, he wrote, "Now Jesus did many other signs in the presence of the disciples, which are not written in this book." Then he went on to say why he had picked out the things that he did write about: "But these are written that you may believe that Jesus is the Christ, the Son of God, and that believing you may have life in his name" (John 20:30-31).

Perhaps long ago when that Roman in the white toga had finished searching through the scroll "according to Mark," and when he had reread that Gospel, he did decide to risk the adventure of faith in Jesus Christ. If so, he would have been baptized and would have sought to share the GOOD NEWS. If he did become a Christian, that Gospel had accomplished its real purpose.

2. How Each Gospel Is Different

At a first reading, all four Gospels in the New Testament seem the same. One part from Luke, for instance, may seem the same as another from Matthew. But the Gospels are not the same. They are not like four copies of the same photograph. As a person gets to know them better, he can say, "That sounds like Mark," or, "That's the way John usually put it." The four Gospels are like four brothers who have the same parents. They look alike, yet each one is different.

Who wrote these Gospels? Almost nothing is known about the authors. None of them signed his name to his work. Each kept himself and his name in the background, as if to say, "This is what all Christians believe. This is the GOOD NEWS as it is taught in the Christian church." The Gospels are not personal books written by authors who wanted to become famous.

In fact, at the beginning of the church there were no Gospels at all. Christians got along quite well simply by remembering what Jesus had said and done. But as the church grew, people far from Palestine became Christian. So it seemed wise to write down some of the things Jesus had said and done. Besides, false teachings appeared and Christians needed a written GOOD NEWS so they could check new teachings to see whether or not they were true. Then, of course, old age and death took away the persons who had known Jesus personally. Neither Jesus nor most of his disciples had written books, so someone else had to do the job of writing down the GOOD NEWS. That is why the first and oldest Gospel was written. It was called the GOOD NEWS "according to Mark."

Mark was written about forty years after Jesus was crucified. At that time Christians were targets of suspicion. They were arrested and condemned to death by the Romans. A cruel sport was made of the executions. The Romans nailed some Christians to crosses, pouring tar over them, and then setting them on fire. They threw others to hungry lions so that the crowd could watch the beasts tear men, women, and children to pieces. The Christians, in their pain and fright, must have wanted to know, "Why? Why must we suffer and die?"

In those times they turned again and again to the Gospel of Mark to read how Jesus met suffering and death. The Christians in Rome liked this Gospel because it is full of action. It pictures Jesus as a doer of deeds, the One, sent by God, who drove out demons, who quieted storms. He did not suffer and die by accident. No, everything that happened to Jesus was according to the will and purpose of God. To the Christians in Rome the vigorous Gospel of Mark said, "Have courage! Jesus, who had power to control even the storms, will bring you the victory."

Another Gospel, which we call Matthew, was written some years later in another city, perhaps Antioch. There a respected Christian teacher collected many sayings of Jesus as they were remembered by the first Christians. He started his Gospel with a family tree for Jesus which goes back to Abraham, the forefather of the Hebrew people. Then he told the story of how Jesus was born in Bethlehem. He collected prophecies from the Old Testament which pointed to Jesus as the Messiah. ("Messiah" is the Hebrew word for Christ.) Often he quoted prophecies from the Old Testament to show that God was at work in all that happened to Jesus. This writer rewrote or copied almost all of the Gospel of Mark. Because he wanted to write a more complete Gospel he added other sayings and deeds of Jesus at places where they seemed to fit best. The Gospel of Matthew tells the GOOD NEWS that God had been preparing for the coming of Jesus ever since the time of Abraham. For those Christians who had been Jews before and who had grown up with the Hebrew Bible, the Gospel "according to Matthew" was a favorite. Many churches wanted to have copies of it.

A third Gospel started with a more ambitious idea than either Mark or Matthew. Luke, a physician, wanted to tell Theophilus, a friend of his, the whole story of how the GOOD NEWS came with Jesus Christ and how it spread as far as the city of Rome. Even a scroll thirty feet long was not big enough for Luke's purpose. So he divided his book into two parts. One part came to be known as the GOOD NEWS "according to Luke." The second part was called the "Acts of the Apostles." The writer collected the accounts of the GOOD NEWS "as they were delivered to us by those who from the beginning were eyewitnesses. . . ." He wrote "an orderly account" for Theophilus. At the beginning of his GOOD NEWS Luke put the family tree of Jesus. He traced it all the way back to Adam, the father of mankind. He wanted to say that the GOOD NEWS is for everyone who is descended from Adam— for all races of men and for all people, even—and especially—

for the poor and despised. Luke's Gospel mentions the poor more often than any other Gospel.

The Gospel of John was the last of the four to be put down on papyrus. It was written by an unnamed man who could say of Jesus: ". . . He came to dwell among us, and we saw his glory, such glory as befits the Father's only Son . . ." (*New English Bible*, John 1:14). This Gospel is not as crowded with sayings and deeds as the other three. It moves more slowly to show how God was hidden in Jesus. This Gospel tells about seven "signs" or miracles which showed the glory of God in Jesus. Because it speaks of the mysterious radiance of God in Jesus and testifies to the eternal life which comes to a believer *now* through Jesus Christ, it is called the "spiritual Gospel." Many persons consider it the most beautiful of the four Gospels. The Gospel of John is like a piece of great music—the more often a person hears it, the more he can find in it.

Mark starts with John the Baptist; Matthew traces a family tree back to Abraham; Luke goes all the way back to Adam. John goes beyond all three. John goes back to God and to the time before the world existed. What John wrote baffles many people. By translating a few key words, the important meaning becomes clearer:

> IN THE BEGINNING—always, before time began
> WAS THE WORD—God, the Son
> AND THE WORD WAS WITH GOD—he was exactly as the Father is and where the Father is
> AND THE WORD WAS GOD . . . AND THE WORD BECAME FLESH—he entered his own world as a baby
> AND DWELT AMONG US—lived on earth as a real human being
> . . . WE HAVE BEHELD HIS GLORY . . . we ourselves have discovered who he really is by his living presence among Christians (John 1:1, 14).

John's story of how the disciples learned to see this hidden glory in Jesus reaches a climax with "doubting Thomas." When Thomas saw the wounded hands of Jesus after the resurrection, he knew that the GOOD NEWS was standing right in front of him. He fell to his knees and cried out, "My Lord and my God!"

3. "Family Album" According to Luke*

The Gospel of Luke has more to say about certain "hidden years" in Jesus' life than any of the other three Gospels. Those were the years *before* Jesus stepped down into the muddy waters of the Jordan to be baptized by the wilderness preacher, John. Only one other Gospel, Matthew, has anything to say about those early years. That is why they are called the "hidden years."

This part of the gospel story in Luke and Matthew becomes a kind of family album. Both Gospels offer a few pictures of the birth and childhood of Jesus.

We can imagine the writer of the Gospel of Luke gathering materials for his book. As he did so, he sorted out sheets of papyrus. Each piece had on it some of the stories or sayings of Jesus. He arranged his materials in an orderly way. The largest stack of papyrus sheets consisted of stories about the last week in Jerusalem. In another collection, Luke gathered pages from a diary which he had kept while traveling with Paul. And in a small heap were some songs that Christians in Palestine often sang. One was the song of Zechariah, the venerable priest who was the father of John the Baptist. Another was the song Mary sang when a heavenly messenger appeared to her and told her, a virgin, that she would give birth to a son who would be called Jesus. The songs are similar in form to the psalms of the Old Testament. The

* Luke's story of what happened before Jesus was born is in Luke 1: 5-80.

early Christians were accustomed to singing psalms, so it was natural that their hymns were psalms also. Like a psalm, the song of Zechariah begins:

> *Blessed be the Lord God of Israel,* (one voice)
> *for he has visited and redeemed his people.* (answering
>   voice)

The ancient Latin name for this song is the *Benedictus* ("blessed"). It is a song of joy which praises God for the fulfillment of his great promises in Jesus.

Many of the first Christians were poor and lowly people. They liked to sing the song of Mary. Its Latin name is the *Magnificat* ("he magnifies"). One of its verses says:

> *He has put down the mighty from their thrones,* (idea "a")
> *and exalted those of low degree;* (idea "b," opposite to "a")
> *he has filled the hungry with good things,* (similar to "b")
> *and the rich he has sent empty away.* (similar to "a")

Along with these songs, Luke included in his Gospel the story of Zechariah and his wife Elizabeth. Elizabeth became a mother in her old age; this was especially God's doing. She was the mother of John, the same John who grew up in the wilderness and came to be known as John the Baptist. The most famous part of Luke's "family album" is the story of the shepherds outdoors at night and of angels in the sky singing:

> *Glory to God in the highest,*
> *and on earth peace. . . .*

In these few words Luke records the great event of Jesus' birth: "She gave birth to her first-born son and wrapped him in swaddling cloths, and laid him in a manger. . . ."

God . . . in a manger! He who moves sun and stars as easily as a man might move pieces on a checkerboard, . . . he who holds the universe in his hand as tenderly as a man might hold a bluebird. . . . That night he lay in the straw of a manger.

Luke also wrote about a mystery that surrounds Jesus' birth. It was a mystery that the early Christians apparently did not talk about very much because it could easily be misunderstood. Jesus was born of a virgin. In later years, Christians recited their belief in this wondrous fact in the words of the creed: ". . . Conceived by the Holy Ghost, Born of the Virgin Mary. . . ." The Gospel of Matthew also speaks of this strange fact, but the other two Gospels have nothing to say about it.

The birth of Jesus is part of the GOOD NEWS which Luke unfolds in his Gospel. In the "family album" part of his Gospel Luke hints at the GOOD NEWS. Jesus' birth was a "sign" of the GOOD NEWS, but only a few persons noticed it at the time.

4. The Census and the "Sign" in Bethlehem

Many people traveled along the high ridge road south from Jerusalem to Bethlehem. To the left of the ridge travelers could look toward the Dead Sea and the brown, wrinkled hills of Moab. To the right they could look down into the green valleys and vineyards. Along that road they could not help noticing the soldiers of Augustus Caesar, emperor at Rome. Soldiers in brightly polished helmets patrolled the road. They turned aside for no one. Everyone else had to move out of the way when they tramped proudly along.

An officer drew his soldiers to attention. "You, you, and you," he barked, pointing at three of them. "Take up positions in Bethlehem."

The officer was well experienced with people who hated foreign soldiers. "Never go out alone," he told his men. "Better three than two together. Watch out for an ambush. Don't let anyone who looks suspicious get behind you. Keep order. Hit first, ask questions later. We must teach these people to respect a Roman soldier!"

Every available soldier was on duty. It was census-taking time at Bethlehem, and soldiers were needed to keep order. Taking

a census was extremely unpopular among the Jewish people. It was like rubbing salt into an open sore. A census meant more taxes—money to build Roman roads and aqueducts, money for the luxurious living of a heathen emperor. The Romans had organized an efficient system to raise taxes. They ordered every Jew to go to his family home. There the tax officials were able to find out exactly who should pay taxes on property which a Jewish family might own in common. Loopholes in collecting taxes could be closed.

Hardly anyone noticed some other travelers on that same road to Bethlehem. These were men shambling along under dirty sheep's wool coats or ragged mantles. Their faces had been burned the color of mahogany by the sun in the wilderness. They were shepherds who scrounged among the barren hills for the last blade of green to feed their flocks.

In those times people looked down on shepherds as some people today may look down on a junk collector. Anybody could take care of dumb sheep. Besides, who would want to spend night after night in the hills, wrapped in a sheep's wool, scratching himself for fleas? Or roast during the day in the hot sun with no one to talk to but a flock of sheep?

Nor was it likely that anyone paid much attention to a carpenter from Nazareth who came along the same road. His name was Joseph, and he walked the eighty miles to Bethlehem with Mary so that he and his betrothed could be listed in the census.

One night, after the soldiers had set up guard posts, after strangers from the north road had bedded down in the inn with their donkeys and camels, and when all was quiet and still, a thin wail sounded in the dark. Few were awake to hear it. It was the cry of a newborn infant in a nearby stable.

The next morning shepherds were seen at the town marketplace. They stammered a strange tale about armies of angels in the night sky. They glorified God in a new psalm of praise. The shepherds claimed that they had seen a *sign*.

"What sign?" the people asked.

The shepherds answered, "Just as the angels said, a baby born in the night."

Curious people went to look at the baby, pink-faced and sleepy. "Why he looks just like any other baby," they said. They shrugged their shoulders and dismissed the shepherds' tale as nonsense.

One day, after standing in line at the census booth in Bethlehem, the carpenter—Joseph of Nazareth—finally came up to the census official. The official bent over his tablet and wrote down the family details. And at the end he wrote,

One child: a boy. Name: JESUS

5. "Family Album" According to Matthew*

The child Jesus was almost murdered.

This is what Matthew's "family album" has to say about the early years of Jesus. Jesus, who one day was to be the Messiah King and rule over the hearts of Christians, was born into deadly danger. Another kind of king, Herod the Great, tried to find the hidden Messiah King to destroy him.

How this happened and how Jesus was rescued and kept safe is the theme of the "family album" story in Matthew's Gospel. On the one side we see the suspicious, uneasy Herod. He plotted to find the hidden king in order to murder him. On the other side were the "wise men" from the east. They came to bring the hidden king costly gifts.

Who were the wise men? The Gospel tells us little about them, saying only that they came from far away and followed the star of a king. They were probably astrologers who believed that the coming of every great person in the world was announced by a

* The account of the wise men and the flight to Egypt is in Matthew 2: 1-23.

star in the sky. This particular star, they said, was the star of Judea, a kingdom in the west.

Astronomers today say that what the wise men may have seen was really a comet or the light of several planets whose orbits came close together in the night sky. These are the speculations of scientists. The Gospel writers were not interested in the kind of astronomical questions which people today might ask. Moreover, the Bible rejects the belief that a person can read in the stars what will happen in the future. The Gospel simply tells how God's hidden and surprising purpose unfolded. Nothing could defeat it. Not even Herod. In contrast to enemies of Jesus in Jerusalem, there were those from faraway lands who came to worship him. The GOOD NEWS of Jesus was gladly received by Gentiles and foreigners. And all the while God, who created the stars, held a shielding hand over the little child Jesus.

Naturally the wise men went to Jerusalem, the biggest city in Judea. They asked questions. Where is the new king? In which palace can we find him? But no one knew about any king other than old Herod—a man who had put three of his sons to death for fear they might topple him from his throne.

Herod heard about the strangers in the city and the rich gifts they were carrying. He heard of their weird notion about a new king so great that a new star had appeared to announce his birth. The old king was afraid, for he was superstitious and a believer in fate. He, Herod, was king of the Jews. And he intended to keep on being king. So Herod called in his scribes. What had the prophets said about a future "Messiah King"? Where would the "King" appear?

The scribes thumbed through holy writings and read what the prophet Micah had written centuries before. From the little village of Bethlehem "shall come a ruler who will govern my people Israel." A thousand years before, the great King David had been born in Bethlehem. In the future a new king would come from Bethlehem, or at least he would be a descendant of David.

This prophecy gave a clue to the astrologers and to Herod. The astrologers acted rapidly. They hurried to Bethlehem, found Jesus, and gave him their gifts. When the wise men did not return to Jerusalem to announce their discovery, Herod sent his soldiers to Bethlehem to get the king. To be sure the boy king could not escape, he ordered the soldiers to kill all male children in Bethlehem who were two years old or less.

Before the soldiers arrived to carry out their cruel errand, Joseph and Mary had left their house and slipped away at night on the road south to Egypt.

Did all this happen by chance? No, says the writer of Matthew's Gospel. He quotes a prophet's saying: "Out of Egypt have I called my son." A few years later when Herod died, it was safe for Joseph and Mary to return. Then they took their son "out of Egypt" and settled in Nazareth.

6. How Jesus Became a Carpenter*

There is only one story about what Jesus said and did as a boy. It is a story that tells how Jesus almost did not become a carpenter.

In Bible times a Jewish boy,became a man when he was twelve years old. At twelve Jesus was big and strong enough to start working with his father, Joseph the carpenter. A carpenter in those days made plows and yokes for farmers. He built furniture and made doors for the stone houses. Often he was a man who could build a bridge, or a boat, or a house. He was used to rough, heavy work, like whipsawing boards out of an oak log.

It was expected that Jesus would become a carpenter, but it almost did not happen.

---

* The account of the boy Jesus in the Temple is told in Luke 2:41-51. Details about Jesus' brothers and sisters are given in Matthew 12:46; 13:55-56.

When Jesus was twelve years old Joseph and Mary went to Jerusalem for the Passover Festival. Jesus went along with them. He was the oldest in a family of five brothers and several sisters. While Jesus was in Jerusalem for the days of the festival he forgot about being a carpenter. He almost forgot what day of the week it was. His mind was filled with a new discovery. He had found the Temple school. In this school were learned men, men who knew much, much more about the holy Books of the Law and the Prophets than did any rabbi in Nazareth.

Hour after hour Jesus talked with them. Here at the Temple was where he wanted to stay. The teachers were ready to welcome him as a bright scholar.

In the synagogue school at Nazareth Jesus had learned to read and write. He had memorized long passages of Scripture. He had thought deeply about the Hebrew Bible and had many questions to ask the wise teachers in the Temple—questions they could not answer. To stay in the Temple—to think and talk about the things of God—this would be his real business.

But it was not to be. The worried parents finally found their missing son and scolded him for forgetting them. Luke's Gospel closes the story with words that speak volumes: "He went . . . to Nazareth, and was obedient to them. . . ."

The only other thing that Luke has to say is: "Jesus increased in wisdom and in stature, and in favor with God and man."

II

PRELUDE TO

PUBLIC MINISTRY

7. How Palestine Became a Roman Province

IN JESUS' DAY it seemed as if the entire world, including Palestine, were under the thumb of the Roman emperor. Palestine was only a small part of the mighty Roman Empire, but this tiny country where Jesus lived had never actually been conquered by the Romans.

Every Jewish boy was taught the long history of his people. For nearly six hundred years before Jesus was born—ever since the Babylonians had leveled Jerusalem to the ground in 586 B.C.— the land of Palestine had been ruled by powerful foreign empires. But in all those years it had remained Jewish. It had not become Persian, or Greek, or Roman. Proudly the Jews remembered a glorious and surprising century when they were free and independent, from 165 to 63 B.C. At that time heroic Jewish fighters set up an independent Jewish state. For a century the Jewish people were independent. Then in the year 63 an embarrassing

thing happened to the Jews. The Pharisees and other strict religious Jews disliked their own corrupt priest-kings so much that
they asked the Romans for help. Pompey, the Roman general,
obliged. He marched in with Roman soldiers. The Romans had
their eyes on Palestine for some time because it was a land bridge
between Europe, Asia, and Africa. With scarcely a battle, the
land of the Jews fell, like a ripe plum, into Roman hands.

At first the Romans governed Palestine indirectly. They simply
picked native rulers to govern the land. One was King Herod
the Great. Herod had the ambition to be a Roman to the Romans
and a Jew to the Jews. The Romans in turn allowed the Jews to
govern themselves in all religious matters. They could worship
as they pleased.

Wherever the Romans extended their empire, they insisted on
law and order. They built paved roads, drove out bandits and
pirates, and fostered business and trade. But often the Romans
were cruel in asserting their power. When the city of Sepphoris
near Nazareth revolted, the Romans crucified a thousand men
from the city and made slaves of the rest of the townspeople.

In 4 B.C. when King Herod the Great died, the Romans split
up his kingdom. For Judea, the trouble spot, they named a new
Roman governor. Other parts of Palestine they put under the
rule of little "kings" called tetrarchs.

The Romans insisted on a steady flow of tax money from
Palestine. In each district they sold the right to collect taxes to
"publicans." Each publican had to guarantee to get the amount of
money the Romans wanted. Whatever was left over, he could
keep for himself as profit. Many of the publicans were ambitious
Jews and were bitterly hated by the people.

The Jews, a proud people, despised all non-Jews, including the
pagan Romans. They had a word for the pagans: they called them
Gentiles or dogs. The Jews felt superior because they believed
that they were the chosen people of God. They were the children
of Abraham and therefore the only heirs to the promises of God.

No Jewish boy was allowed to forget the honor of being a Jew and belonging to the chosen people.

In this world Jesus grew up. What did he think of the Romans? According to the gospel story, Jesus did not share the bitter and fanatic hatred of Jew for Gentile, of Jew for Roman overlord. When he was asked whether it was right to pay taxes to the Romans, Jesus asked for a coin. "Whose picture is stamped on this coin?" he asked. There was no question. On the coin appeared the head of Caesar with a wreath around his brow. "Give to Caesar what belongs to him," said Jesus, "and to God what belongs to him."

The Gospels also tell us that some Roman soldiers were friendly to the Jews. One Roman officer had built a fine synagogue for the Jews in Capernaum. Indeed, a Roman centurion once asked Jesus to heal his favorite slave.

8. Who the Sadducees and Pharisees Were

It was not practical for the Romans to recruit Jews for the army. A Jew would not work on the Sabbath. If there were a battle on the Sabbath, the Romans knew that Jewish soldiers would not fight. Nor would the Jews march under the brass Roman eagles which the army carried on poles like flags. To the Jews the eagles were forbidden "graven images."

The Jews were intensely religious. But they had different ways of being religious. Among the Jews in the time of Jesus were several religious groups. The most important were the Sadducees, the Pharisees, and the priests and Levites. Another important group was the Essenes, but they are not mentioned by name in the Gospels.

Sadducee was the name of a large group of Jewish families which proudly claimed to be descendants of Zadok, a priest of David. These families of priests and their members had become wealthy because they controlled the Temple. The Sadducees chose the high priest. They collected all the taxes for the Temple. Every Jew was required to pay the Temple tax; Jews in all parts of the world paid this tax regularly. In this way the Temple became the richest treasury in Palestine. The Sadducees also controlled the selling of oxen and sheep for the many thousands of sacrifices in the Temple. From each sale they made a profit.

The Sadducees were conservative in religion and in politics. In religion they accepted as their Bible only the first five Books of the Law: Genesis, Exodus, Leviticus, Numbers, and Deuteronomy. They rejected the new teaching about the resurrection from the dead and refused to believe in angels simply because there was no proof in these books that there is a resurrection or that angels exist. Politically, the Sadducees wanted peace and quiet in the land. They did not want to anger the Romans. They wanted to keep things just as they were. They mistrusted and feared any fanatic who might cause a disturbance. The Sadducees controlled the Sanhedrin. This was a council of seventy which governed the religious affairs of the Jewish people.

As long as the Temple stood and daily sacrifices were offered there, the Sadducees were rich and powerful. But Jesus predicted that the time would come when the Temple would be completely destroyed. Not one stone would be left on top of another. Talk like this was sure to disturb the Sadducees.

The Sadducees were the aristocrats among the priests, but there were also other families of priests. These were the descendants of Levi and were called Levites. In Jesus' time there were literally thousands of priests in these families. There were so many priests that they had to take turns serving in the Temple. A priest might not have to serve more than one or two weeks a year. Among the priests was Zechariah, the father of John the Baptist. When the Christian church began, some of the priests became Christians.

The professional priests and the aristocratic Sadducees were usually born into their positions. There were other Jews who voluntarily joined a religious group of strict, serious-minded lay-men. These were the Pharisees. They liked to quote a saying that if all the people would keep the Sabbath perfectly, the Messiah would come. The problem was exactly how should a Jew keep the Sabbath. The law said, "Do no work on the Sabbath." But what was work?

Was it work to gargle one's throat on a Sabbath?

Was it right to eat an egg laid on a Sabbath? Surely the hen had worked to lay it.

How many steps could one take without "working"?

The Pharisees pondered these questions seriously. They wanted to become truly righteous people in the sight of God. They were determined to do all they could to obey God's laws. So they classified all the laws in the Holy Scriptures. They listed the "laws of Moses" and came to a grand total of 613 laws. A man who fears God, they said, is a man who keeps every one of these laws. A man who breaks or neglects any one of them is a sinner.

Keeping these laws was not a simple matter. All kinds of questions came up about the meaning of the laws. So the Pharisees went to work and collected the interpretations of the laws as spoken by famous rabbis. These interpretations answered questions like the one about how many steps a person is permitted to walk on a Sabbath without "working."

Not only did a God-fearing Jew have to keep the 613 laws, but he could also never associate with a sinner. A religious man had to keep himself separate. The word Pharisee means "a separate people."

Many Pharisees were prosperous businessmen and merchants. They were rich enough so that they could afford to be religious. A poor man could not afford to worry about eating an egg laid on a Sabbath, for example. He did not have time to study every detail of the hundreds of laws.

Some Pharisees quit business and became experts in the laws of Moses. They were called "lawyers" or simply "scribes." They kept the Books of the Law and classified and wrote down hundreds of interpretations of the Law. They had the education which was required to be strictly religious. The Gospels often mention scribes and Pharisees in one breath. The two depended on each other and worked closely together.

The Sadducees managed the Temple, but the Pharisees managed the synagogues. They decided who should be allowed to worship there. Nothing worse could happen to a Jew than to be excluded from the synagogue. The Pharisees wanted to build a "fence of the law" around the Jewish people which would be so strong that everyone would be guided to obey all the laws of God.

Being a Pharisee tended to make a person proud and narrow-minded. Pharisees liked to say long prayers in the marketplace to show off their piety. They were extremely careful to give a tenth of all they had to the Temple. Jesus noticed how a Pharisee would even give a tenth of his anise and cummin (garden herbs something like parsley).

Because they were so earnest about religion and so devoted to the will of God, some Pharisees became Christians. Nicodemus and Paul, for example, were Pharisees.

9. A Revolution Ready to Explode

Living in the world in which Jesus grew up was like watching a fuse sputter and burn, waiting for it to explode like a bomb. The Jewish people were on edge. They were humiliated to be ruled by Romans who worshiped graven images. They looked back longingly to the glory of King David and King Solomon. More often they looked to the future and expected great things to happen.

"The time will come," they said, "when God will keep his promises of old and will send us a Messiah to establish his kingdom."

What will the kingdom be like?

What will the Messiah do?

To these questions the people of Jesus' day had many different answers. Some expected the Messiah to come like a heroic general on a white horse. He would lead the armies of his people from victory to victory. He would destroy the Romans and make Jerusalem the capital of the world.

Others thought of a glorious new age that would begin when the Messiah came. The whole world would change. There would no longer be war. The lion and the lamb would live at peace with each other. The poor would have plenty to eat. The fields would bear abundant crops of wheat and olives and grapes.

Still others thought of the Messiah as a second Moses— a great lawgiver. He would establish righteousness and justice in all the world.

Although people had so many different ideas about the Messiah, they all agreed that when the Messiah would come, the rule of the hated Roman overlords would end. Some wanted to hurry matters along and strike immediately. They were the Zealots who talked riot and revolution. They wanted to drive the Romans into the sea and to rid the land of the foreign oppressor.

Jesus lived in a time when any new word about the Messiah or the kingdom of God would draw excited crowds.

10. Excitement in the Desert*

When Jesus was thirty years old, the stirring news spread through all the land: "A prophet of the Highest has come." People were talking about a man who lived like a second Elijah. He had refused to live in a house in town or village, and had grown up in

* Matthew 3:1-17 and Luke 3:1-18, 21-22 give an account of the work of John the Baptist and the baptism of Jesus.

the desert. He did not eat food from the farmer's field; he ate the wild honey and grasshoppers of the desert hills. He wore rough camel-hair garments. He feared no man, and his words were like fire. Not since the days of Amos and Elijah had a man spoken with such power. For four hundred years, since the time of Malachi, there had been no prophet.

This man of the desert was John. People called him "John the baptizer" because he washed people in the river in a rite of repentance from sin. But why would anyone want to be washed in the Jordan by a wild-looking man like John?

Such washing was not unknown to the Jews. Any *Gentile* who wanted to become a Jew had to be baptized first. But such baptism was never necessary for a born Jew who had been properly circumcised as an infant.

Crowds came to see the prophet in the wilderness. They were awestruck and stayed to listen, though what he said made them shiver with fear.

"The time is now!" thundered John. He declared that the Jews were like a barren olive tree. God has taken up the ax already, he said, and he will come to chop through the roots. When the tree topples, he will throw it into the fire. Not in the distant future, but right now!

John made himself very clear. God is coming with a winnowing fork in his hand. He will gather the bundles of wheat to thresh it by trampling on it. The few kernels of wheat he will save, but the great mountain of chaff (the husks) he will burn in unquenchable fire.

People understood this picture language very well. The ax at the root, the fire for the chaff, this meant that God was coming to judge his people. He will send his Messiah to separate the good from the bad, the faithful from the unfaithful. This might happen very soon—in a few days, perhaps in a few hours!

"Get ready!" John would whisper, and the people strained to listen. "Repent of your sins! Change your minds and hearts! As a sign of your change, come and be washed (baptized) in the Jordan. Make yourselves ready to be saved like the kernels of wheat on the threshing floor."

No one doubted that John was a man of God. Even the skeptical Sadducees did not dare deny that. Jesus himself said, later on, that there had never been a man born who was greater than John.

As the Gospel of Matthew makes clear, not even John fully understood what the Messiah would be or do. He did not understand that the Messiah would be a humble man who would suffer for his people. He did not understand that the Messiah would come not to condemn men but to save them by suffering and dying for them.

At the very time Jesus stood among the crowds, listening to John, there were some who held their hands over their mouths and muttered, "That man, John, he must be the Messiah himself!"

John heard these rumors and his eyes flashed. "No!" he said. John declared that he was not even worthy to untie the Messiah's sandals as a slave might do for his master.

Then John spied some of the richly dressed Sadducees in the back of the crowd. "You brood of snakes!" he said, pointing straight at them. The people were astonished at such bold words. This made them all the more sure that John was really a prophet. Many thought he was Elijah himself, returned from heaven into which he had vanished in a fiery chariot centuries ago.

Then came the dramatic moment when Jesus and John stood face to face. Jesus stepped out of the crowd. He laid aside his mantle at the water's edge, bowed his head, and asked to be baptized. John shrank back. "I need to be baptized by you," he protested.

Jesus simply said, "Let it be so now."

Then Jesus added words that hint at the meaning of his baptism. "For thus it is fitting for us to fulfill all righteousness." This is the only explanation the Gospels give for this strange baptism.

One thing should be clear. Jesus did not come to be baptized because of any sin. It was true that even soldiers and tax collectors were coming to be baptized by John. They wanted forgiveness for the sins that weighed so heavily on their consciences. Jesus, however, was as the first Christians declared, "in every respect . . . tempted as we are, yet without sinning" (Hebrews 4:15). Jesus was sinless. He did not need to be forgiven. What he meant when he talked to John about "fulfilling all righteousness" was simply, "I must do everything that God requires of everybody else." Jesus became part of the people, humbly and quietly. He did not stand apart from the human race.

Looking back at the life of Jesus from his baptism to his resurrection, it can also be said that in his baptism Jesus took the way that would lead to the cross where he would die for the sins of the world. But at the moment, all this was hidden and veiled from human eyes.

It was hidden from John particularly. He protested: "I need to be baptized by you."

Jesus answered that he wanted to be baptized along with all the others. As Jesus waded into the deep water, he had no doubt that what he insisted on doing was right. Suddenly it was as if the heavens opened and the power of the Spirit flashed down upon him like the swoop of a white-winged dove in the sun. Ringing in Jesus' ears was a heavenly voice that echoed words of Psalm 2 and Isaiah 42:

> THOU ART MY BELOVED SON; WITH THEE I AM WELL
> PLEASED.

It was a tremendous spiritual experience for Jesus. Years ago in the Temple when he was twelve, he had said, "my Father." Now he heard the voice of God in the language of Scripture saying, *"You are my Son."*

11. The Greatest Enemy of Jesus*

Did the Devil appear to Jesus in the desert like a half-animal, half-human thing with horns and hooves and a tail?

Nowhere in the gospel story does Jesus describe the Devil in detail at all. In fact, the Bible does not describe the Devil in detail at all. It says nothing about "horns." And since Jesus was all alone in the wilderness with the Devil, there was no one else to observe what happened. Instead, at some unnamed time, Jesus took the disciples aside and told them what had happened in the wilderness.

It can never be known whether or not Jesus actually saw the Devil standing before him as some sort of grisly being. What is known is that the Devil can appear in many forms. He may even appear as an "angel of light," that is, in the form of a very handsome and good being. What is more terrible, the Devil can enter the innermost thoughts of a person. He tries to influence a person through his mind and spirit. He does his work without appearing in visible form.

Another word the Bible uses for the Devil is "the Satan." It means "the adversary" or "the accuser." He is *The Enemy*. The Satan is the greatest enemy of all human beings just as he was Jesus' most terrible enemy.

Why did the Devil come to Jesus right after the baptism by John? Jesus did not explain, but there was an inner connection. After hearing the heavenly voice at his baptism, Jesus had to make a decision. He knew now that he was the Messiah, the person whom God declared to be his "beloved Son." But he did not know what he should do as the Messiah. He had to decide.

The decision he had to make was the most important one in his life. The Devil knew this. He sought to destroy Jesus' work by controlling the decision Jesus had to make.

---

* One account of Jesus' temptation in the wilderness is in Matthew 4: 1-11.

Jesus had no one to go to for help. He could not talk over his problem with trusted friends. He knew that none of the wise teachers in the Temple could help. Not even John the Baptist could tell him what he needed to know.

Instead, Jesus was led "by the Spirit" into the empty wilderness. There he spent a long time—the biblical forty days—thinking, praying, fighting thoughts that might lead him astray, struggling to find the true will of God. Those were days of a great spiritual battle. We may suppose that later when Jesus taught his disciples to pray, "Lead us not into temptation, but deliver us from evil," he was thinking about his terrible temptation during those days in the wilderness.

In the desert Jesus fought against the Devil, but he could not get rid of his great enemy. He had to contend with the Devil's temptations at many other times. The Devil tempted Jesus when men wanted to make him a king. That happened after his miraculous feeding of the multitude. The Devil opposed Jesus on the mountain of the Transfiguration when Peter suggested that the disciples stay there. Peter wanted to remain longer with the shining figures of Moses and Elijah. Again the Devil tempted Jesus on the cross when Jesus' enemies said to him, "He saved others, he cannot save himself." They dared Jesus to come down from the cross in divine power. There must have been many other times when the Devil tempted Jesus.

Here in the wilderness, before Jesus began his ministry, the Devil tempted Jesus in a special way. Jesus did not tell his disciples exactly how. But he did help them to remember what he told them by telling the story of three temptations. Each temptation is described in picture language, and without any long explanations. The gospel story allows the reader to figure out what the story means. This much is clear: the Devil tempted Jesus in a special way, a way that would not be a temptation for anyone except the Messiah. The Devil tempted Jesus to be another kind of Messiah, not the Messiah God wanted him to be.

THE SPIRIT IMMEDIATELY DROVE HIM OUT
INTO THE WILDERNESS.
AND HE WAS IN THE WILDERNESS FORTY DAYS,
TEMPTED BY SATAN;
AND HE WAS WITH THE WILD BEASTS;
AND THE ANGELS MINISTERED TO HIM.

Be a Messiah who can do miracles and feed the hungry! In a land where there was not enough food for all, such a Messiah would soon have thousands of followers. In a few weeks he could win such power that he could sweep away any army that might come against him. Would it not also be a kind and good thing to feed the starving?

Jesus rejected this temptation with a verse he had learned as a boy, from the Hebrew Bible. "Man shall not live by bread alone. . . ." Even if a person has plenty to eat and money in the bank, he is not necessarily closer to God. Probably he is farther from God!

Be a Messiah who can sail out into space and not be hurt! The Jewish people expected the Messiah to show himself by an unmistakable sign. Once a man named Theudas led a great mass of people into the Jordan. He claimed to be the Messiah and promised to divide the water so that they could cross with dry feet. This would be the "sign" of a Messiah. But before Theudas could perform his miracle, the Romans massacred the entire multitude.

The Devil suggested the kind of miracle which would astonish people. They would have to believe in Jesus if he could do something as dramatic as stepping off a high building and floating down unharmed. It would be just the kind of spectacular miracle that would impress people.

Jesus knew, however, that God did not make man to float down from a pinnacle. "You shall not tempt the Lord your God," he said. He could never be a Messiah by trying to test God.

Be a Messiah by using any power to get control over the kingdoms of the world! Perhaps the Devil meant, "Use force—like the power of chariots and armies." Or he may have meant, "Use cunning—like thinking up shrewd schemes to mastermind a powerful underground movement against the Roman Empire." It would all be for a good cause. It would bring all the world to the Messiah!

Jesus knew that even if he held all the power of emperors and kings in his hands, he would not have power over sin. He knew that one must trust God and rely upon him.

What other things happened in the bone-white desert hills when Jesus met his greatest enemy, we will never know. Jesus said no more about it, but we know that the Devil could not defeat Jesus. The GOOD NEWS of the Gospels is that Jesus Christ is stronger than the most dreadful enemy mankind has. In the end Jesus Christ will win the victory.

12. The Best Friends of Jesus*

John the Baptist was so bold and outspoken that he was sure to get into trouble. He spoke out against the high and mighty. He denounced the sinful life of the king, Herod Antipas. The day came when the king arrested him. Finally Herod ordered John's head cut off to please a dancing girl. The news of John's death spread dismay among those who trusted him as a new prophet of God.

According to the Gospel of Mark, John's imprisonment was a signal to Jesus to begin a public ministry. Hearing the news about John, Jesus laid aside his carpenter's hammer and chisel, closed up his shop, and stepped out to preach. Now that John's voice had been silenced, Jesus took his place. He preached the same message: "The kingdom of God is at hand . . . repent!"

It was a message about the kingdom of God that Jesus preached, but he became a very different kind of proclaimer. John had stayed in the desert, but Jesus went into the villages. John ate the sparse food of the wilderness, but Jesus remained

* There are several accounts in the Gospels of the call of the disciples. Two of them are John 1:35-51 and Luke 5:1-11. The names of the Twelve are given in Matthew 10:1-4 and Luke 6:13-16.

with people. In Galilee and Judea he was invited to enjoy the bounty of a wedding feast and other fine meals. John had frightened the people with his words about judgment and doom. Jesus spoke in a different way. He called the poor and lowly to come to him in a way that made men love him.

In one thing Jesus and John were alike. Both gathered disciples. And like John, Jesus also preached "in the power of the Spirit." He brought a message that came not from man but from God.

When people had gone to hear John in the wilderness, they had listened to news about a Messiah who would come soon. When they came to hear Jesus, they heard nothing about a future Messiah. Instead, they heard a new kind of preaching. "The kingdom of God is here!" This was hard to understand. Years later, Christians understood more clearly what Jesus meant. The kingdom of God was in the person of Jesus himself. His presence was the kingdom of God in action. This is the GOOD NEWS, but not everyone could understand it. Many rejected it.

Jesus needed help to proclaim the GOOD NEWS. He wrote no books, but he did need trusted men to carry on the work he began. The Gospels tell several stories about how Jesus gathered his disciples and what kind of men they were. Some were fishermen. One was a tax collector.

This group of men was a happy one. Two brothers were always making so much noise that Jesus called them "sons of thunder." Another man Jesus called "the rock," which is what the name Peter means. Simon was Peter's real name; Simon Peter simply means "Simon, the Rock." The company of the disciples was such a friendly and jolly one that people often invited the whole crowd with Jesus to parties and feasts.

It was no accident that these men became disciples of Jesus. Nor was it an accident that there were just twelve. Jesus picked certain men to be disciples. He would look into a man's eyes and say, "Follow me." Later on Jesus explained, "You did not choose me, but I chose you." Each one of the disciples knew that Jesus had selected him even before he (the disciple) knew anything about it. These men were called disciples because the word "disciple" means a learner. They learned from a teacher who used no books, no desks, and no blackboards. His "school" was the outdoors, or the marketplace, or a house—anywhere he happened to be.

And Jesus chose just twelve men. The number twelve is significant. Every Hebrew knew that this was the number of the tribes of Israel, the chosen people of God. The number twelve is a way of saying what the GOOD NEWS is. It means that Jesus is gathering a people to himself to be the new Israel, the new people of God. The new Israel began with twelve men in Galilee. It would expand to include every Christian on earth.

There were other disciples, also. Jesus had many followers; the Gospels mention a group of seventy. Many persons, including several women, were regarded as followers of Jesus. The Twelve, however, are sometimes called the apostles. "Apostle" means one who is commissioned or sent.

III

JESUS IN

THE PUBLIC EYE

13. When Jesus' Neighbors Tried to Kill Him*

ONE COULD SEE THE VILLAGE of Nazareth from far away across the wheat fields of the Plain of Esdraelon. The houses of Nazareth, set on a hillside, looked like a flock of sheep climbing to the top of the hill. In a village like Nazareth, everybody knew everything about everybody else. The people of the village were like one large family. They knew everything about Mary's household, about the five sons, about the eldest son, Jesus, the carpenter.

Jesus' mother and his brothers were worried. Jesus had been away from home for a long time—out in the wilderness of Judea with John the Baptist, people said. Disturbing tales about Jesus drifted back to Nazareth. He was no longer a working carpenter. He was acting like a teacher of the things of heaven. He even had disciples like a great rabbi. And like a doctor of the Torah, he was preaching in the synagogues. People asked, "Who does that carpenter think he is?"

That was not the half of it. He could be seen sitting comfortably at a table, eating lamb stew from the same bowl with tax gatherers and drinking from the cup they passed around! He was not particular about the company he kept, so it seemed. Nor did he keep the Sabbath with the holy strictness of the honorable Pharisees.

Jesus' brothers and his mother thought that the eldest son was out of his mind. They went to talk to Jesus in another village. They found where he was, but such a crowd had jammed the house that they couldn't get near him. So they sent a message to ask him to come out. Jesus refused. He said his brothers and sisters were right there in front of him—the crowd drinking in his words as eagerly as a horse drinks water after a long, hot day.

All this made the neighbors in Nazareth itch with curiosity. They listened eagerly to every new story about Jesus. They may have heard about the woman who had suffered from a hemorrhage for years. The poor woman, ashamed of her unpleasant ailment, crept through the crowd to get near Jesus. She touched him when he was not looking and from that moment she was clean and healed! There seemed to radiate from this man a *power* that no one had ever seen before.

This news disturbed and unsettled the people of Nazareth. Where did that *power* come from? Why didn't the carpenter come and show it to his neighbors in Nazareth? There were doubtless plenty of people to heal in Nazareth—a deaf and dumb girl, a farmer's wife whose leg had stiffened, an old man whose hands shook so that he had to be fed like a baby, a little girl who cried day and night because of a pain in her abdomen.

"Let him come here and show us what he can do!" gossiped the women at the well of Nazareth. "Why doesn't he help his old friends at home?"

* Accounts of Jesus' rejection in Nazareth can be found in Luke 4:16-30 and Mark 6:1-6.

And one day Jesus came back to Nazareth. A crowd of young men came with him. Sometimes they were refused shelter because one of them had been a tax collector. No matter, they did not mind sleeping under the stars.

People expected wonderful things to happen when he came. Instead, nothing happened. No *power*. As far as the neighbors could see, Jesus couldn't even remove a wart from a boy's hand. (He did heal a few sick folks, but nothing impressive happened.)

Then on the Sabbath Jesus went to the synagogue like any other devout "son of the law." The synagogue was a large, white-washed room. At one side was a wooden lattice and behind it sat the women and little children. The old men sat in front on the seats of honor. Barefoot boys and youths crowded together in the back.

In the front of the room was a seven-branched candlestick and a cabinet in which the scrolls of the Law and the Prophets were kept. A synagogue had no minister or regular preacher, but everyone knew what to do. First an old man got up and said a prayer. It was always very solemn and very long; the longer it was, the more proper it was. Then came the reading from the Books of the Law as it had been done since the days of Ezra long ago. There was a different section to read each Sabbath, and seven men took turns reading the selection for the day. The rule was that each man had to *read*. He could not simply recite the words from memory, holding the scroll in his hands like a child pretending to read.

After the Law came a reading from the Prophets. Jesus gave a signal to the elders. He wanted to be allowed to read. The elders nodded to him. The women leaned nearer the lattice to see. The boys in the back stopped wriggling. The congregation almost stopped breathing. Jesus drew a prayer shawl over his head—it was the proper thing to do—and went forward.

After the regular passage from the Prophets had been read, the reader could choose any other book or passage he wished. Jesus asked for Isaiah. An attendant respectfully handed him the thick roll of Isaiah, the prophet. Jesus opened it. He began with Chapter 61:

> *The Spirit of the Lord is upon me,*
> *because he has anointed me to preach the good news*
>   *to the poor. . . .*

As Jesus read, the lips of the old men moved with his lips. They knew every word by heart. At a certain point Jesus stopped. He did not read the entire passage. He closed the scroll and sat down on the preacher's chair. It was customary in the synagogue for the reader to explain the text. Jesus had read the ancient Hebrew. Now he spoke in the familiar Aramaic dialect of Galilee.

The people in the synagogue relaxed. Their carpenter was doing fine. He had many good things to say about the words of Isaiah. Somehow they did not notice the bombshell which Jesus had dropped into their midst when he announced, "Today this scripture *has been fulfilled* in your hearing." Maybe they thought it was a slip of the tongue, a mistake. Perhaps they thought Jesus meant to say, "will soon be fulfilled" (when the Messiah comes). They marveled how their carpenter could talk for an hour and not run out of anything to say. They commented to each other in low voices and whispers, for in those days it was not unusual for people to chat in the synagogue during the service.

If Jesus had stopped then, nothing would have happened. His brothers would have come up and congratulated him. People would have said, "I enjoyed your sermon." The old men would have stroked their beards approvingly.

But Jesus did not stop. He only paused. Then he looked straight into the eyes of his neighbors. They stopped whispering. He knew what they were thinking. "Why doesn't he show his *power* in his home town if he can show it in Capernaum?" Jesus told them why. He told them so plainly that they could not misunderstand.

Jesus began by talking about the great and famous prophet Elijah. Everyone knew the story of Elijah by heart. From their village the people of Nazareth could see Mount Carmel where Elijah had fought against the prophets of Baal eight hundred years before. "There were many widows in Israel in the days of Elijah," Jesus said, "in the days of the great famine." Then Jesus made his point. "Elijah was sent to none of them but only to Zarephath, in the land of Sidon." Sidon was a harbor town up north in the country of the Gentiles. No one believed in the prophet of God in his home country, but in heathen Sidon a foreign widow took Elijah into her home and trusted in him.

The old men started from their seats. "Blasphemy!" they hissed. "Blasphemy" because Jesus had boldly compared himself to Elijah.

Jesus did not stop. He went on and talked about Elisha who cured Naaman, the foreigner, of leprosy. He did not cure a single leper in Israel. Now the younger men rose from their seats. They shoved the disciples out of the synagogue into the street. Then they rushed for the man in the preacher's chair.

There was only one thing to do with a blasphemer—he must be stoned to death! It must never be said that the people of Nazareth allowed blasphemy in their synagogue!

First they would throw him from the cliff. They would bury his body under stones. Then they would beg the Almighty to forgive the village for welcoming a loathsome blasphemer.

The screaming mob got as far as the cliff. Jesus did not fight back. Nor did the disciples. It was time now for someone to push the carpenter over the edge of the cliff. No one stepped forward to do so. Why, none could explain.

Calmly Jesus walked through the crowd and on down the hill. As he walked away in the sunshine, his figure grew smaller and smaller in the distance. They saw him take the road northeast toward Capernaum.

Years later, when the evangelist began writing the Gospel of John, he put down these words:

He came to his own home, and his own people received him not.

AND THEY ROSE UP
    AND PUT HIM OUT OF THE CITY,
AND LED HIM TO THE BROW OF THE HILL
    ON WHICH THEIR CITY WAS BUILT,
THAT THEY MIGHT THROW HIM DOWN HEADLONG.

14. People in Whom Devils Lived*

Capernaum was a busy and lively city. The main highway from Jerusalem to Damascus passed through Capernaum as it skirted the northern shore of the Sea of Galilee. Every day caravans of traders and freight carriers passed through the city. Many stopped to spend the night. A garrison of Roman soldiers was stationed in Capernaum. People got used to seeing tall, blond Germans or swarthy Spaniards among the soldiers, for they were recruited from the far corners of the empire. They brought many new ideas to the city. Capernaum was also a fishing center. The stone piers at the waterfront smelled of fish as did the barrels of brine in which fish were pickled for export.

Whenever Jesus was in the city, there was still more stir and excitement. The Gospels call Capernaum "his own city" because Jesus made it his headquarters. Probably he stayed in Peter's house. The news about this healer and teacher spread from Capernaum to all the villages in the hills of Galilee.

People had plenty to talk about. Even if they could not understand all that Jesus said each Sabbath in the synagogue, they knew one thing. They knew he did not talk like any other teacher they had ever heard. A Jewish rabbi usually began with a text from the Law of Moses. Then he would read off or recite what Rabbi Eleazar in Babylon had said, and what Rabbi Jochanan had said about what Rabbi Eleazar said, and then what Rabbi Hillel had said about Rabbi Jochanan about Rabbi Eleazar.

"This man, Jesus of Nazareth," people said, "speaks as one who has authority, not as the scribes speak."

Jesus spoke out very plainly. He told the people directly what the will of God was. He was not a man of many books, quotations, proofs, complicated arguments.

---

* Mark 1:23-28 is an account of Jesus healing a man with an unclean spirit.

Jesus not only spoke with authority. He also acted with a *power* that made a person feel as if he stood close to the Holy of Holies in the Temple in Jerusalem. Many stories were told of that *power*.

One Sabbath a man jumped up in the synagogue. He drew in his breath, and then a fearful yell was wrenched from his body as if against his will. His face flushed dark red and he fell to the floor, foaming at the mouth. His body became as stiff as a piece of dried fish. The people next to him shrank back. They were afraid even to wipe the spittle off the man's face.

"An unclean spirit lives in him," they said.

In those days people had other explanations than we have to account for diseases of the body and disturbances of the mind. A common explanation was that the air was full of thousands of spirits or demons. It was said that one could not push a needle into the air without touching a demon. These demons might enter a person's body and cause him to act in weird and frightening ways. Everyone regarded this as a satisfactory way to explain why an afflicted person might act in peculiar ways. For example, a person might not know who he really was and go around thinking he was Alexander the Great, or he might hear voices and see things that weren't there. A demon might make a man shout and seem violent and dangerous, as did the man in the synagogue.

Disturbances like these are explained today as due to epilepsy or some form of mental illness. There are hospitals today for helping the mentally ill. Medical science has found ways to cure many diseases of body and mind, but there are still mysteries of mind and body which physicians and scientists cannot understand.

People were afraid of that man lying on the synagogue floor, but Jesus helped him. He quieted the man's twitching body with a word of command to the "spirit" that was thought to be in him. The Gospels tell many stories of how Jesus helped persons who today might be called maniacs, or epileptics, or mentally ill.

What did it all mean? What lay behind Jesus' power to heal? The Gospel of Matthew has a clear, short answer. If Jesus casts

out demons by the Spirit of God, then—
THE KINGDOM OF GOD HAS COME UPON YOU!
Each story of Jesus and the people in whom demons lived was a
sign that One more mighty had come, One who was stronger than
the weirdest, most frightening, most mysteriously evil thing that
can bring suffering to a man's mind and body.

15. People with a Dread Disease*

There is a disease which starts with a thickening of the skin. In
time swellings appear and the sense of feeling in fingers or toes
disappears. The flesh begins to rot and bones of the hand, or foot,
or face soften, then fall away. Today this sickness is called Hansen's disease or, more commonly, leprosy. In Jesus' day this disease and many other skin diseases that seemed to be the same
were all called leprosy. What the Bible calls leprosy may have
been Hansen's disease in some cases. More often it was probably
some kind of chronic skin disease like ringworm, eczema, or skin
ulcers.

The laws of Moses which the Jews observed were very strict
in matters of sanitation and hygiene. The Jews were a very clean
people. If anyone had a skin disease, he had to show it to the
priests who were the medical officers of that time. The priests had
to decide whether the sick person was "clean" or "unclean." Usually, the priests ordered a seven-day quarantine. If, after that time
the disease did not get better, the sick person was declared to be
"unclean" or even a "leper." He was no longer allowed to live in
the village.

Such an unfortunate person was required to wear torn clothes.
He was not allowed to wear anything on his head so that everyone could recognize him as "unclean." People called him a leper

* Mark 1:40-45 is an account of how Jesus healed a leper.

and avoided getting near him or touching him. The leper suffered not only from his disease but also from being an outcast. Little children were warned to run away whenever they saw a leper.

Jesus, however, did not shrink back when he saw a leper; nor did he draw to the side of the path to avoid him. One day a leper came toward him. The ragged man knelt humbly in the dust. "If you will, you can make me clean," he said.

Jesus had done no miracles of healing in Nazareth because his neighbors only wanted him to show off. They did not believe in him. But where there was faith, even if only a little, Jesus was ready to help. He healed the leper and asked him to keep it a secret.

Just how could a leper keep such a secret? He could not. He had to tell everyone about the man who healed him.

Crowds who heard the leper's story came to see Jesus. Jesus could not enter any village by daylight without being mobbed. He had to stay in the country, and even there he had no peace.

16. Unexpected Faith*

The leper who asked Jesus to heal him was a Jew. He believed in the God of Abraham, Isaac, and Jacob.

But in Capernaum there were other men who worshiped Mars, the Roman god of war and violence, or Venus, the goddess of love and sex, or Isis, the great deity of Egypt, or dozens of other gods. They were the Roman soldiers in the garrison. Their commanding officer was a hard, tough centurion. He maintained strict discipline. "Shine up the chariots," he barked. If the chariots did not pass inspection the next day, it would be a terrible day for the garrison. The centurion expected and got obedience.

---

* Matthew 8:5-13 is an account of Jesus and the centurion. A similar story is told in John 4:46-54 as the second "sign" that Jesus performed.

After living so long among the Jews, the Roman centurion had learned a good deal about the Jewish religion. Like a few other Romans, he had become very interested in the simple, dignified faith of the Jews. He wanted to know more about the one God who was never pictured in human form.

Even though it was known that the centurion was interested in the religion of the Jews, it amazed even Jesus when that officer went out of his way to meet him at the gate of the city. The proud Roman asked for help. He told Jesus that his favorite slave was paralyzed with a deadly illness. Would Jesus help?

"I will come and heal him," Jesus said instantly.

The officer was trained to think fast and to make up his mind quickly. He did not want Jesus to disgrace himself by entering a pagan house.

"Only say the word," the army officer begged.

Jesus dismissed the centurion with a kindly word. "Go; be it done for you as you have believed."

To his disciples Jesus exclaimed, "Not even in Israel have I found such faith!"

The people of Israel believed that only they were God's chosen people. They were sure that God's promises were meant especially for the sons of Abraham. God would send his Messiah to deliver them. But the GOOD NEWS in Jesus is that the promises of God are for *all people.*

17. Unexpected Forgiveness*

Whenever Jesus came to Capernaum on a Sabbath, there were many who wanted to bring their sick to him to be healed. This could not be done on a Sabbath as all work was forbidden. So

---

* Luke 5:17-26 and Mark 2:1-12 give accounts of the healing of the paralytic.

they waited until sundown, the hour when the Sabbath ended. At sunset, a wretched parade lined up to see Jesus—people whose bodies were covered with ulcers, little children with thin arms and swollen bellies, men with sightless eyes, mothers who suffered with the aftereffects of childbirth.

In this scene the Gospels picture the "good news to the poor . . . and recovering of sight to the blind." These were the words of Isaiah which Jesus had read in the synagogue at Nazareth. These words came true in what Jesus did and was.

Jesus did not heal every sick person in Capernaum, but he healed so many that the enthusiastic townspeople wanted him to stay in their city permanently. Jesus explained that he could not stay because he had to travel to all the other towns of Galilee to announce the kingdom of heaven. He and his disciples set out to travel from village to village.

There were times when Jesus felt it necessary to withdraw from the crowds of curious folk. Then he would go to the desert where he could be sure of being alone. He spent hours, perhaps days, in prayer.

By this time reports of what Jesus was doing had reached the Temple in Jerusalem. A delegation of religious experts came northward to Capernaum to investigate Jesus. Since they were important and dignified men, they were given the seats of honor inside the house where Jesus was preaching. Soon the house was packed with people. People who could not get in jammed the narrow alley outside and craned their necks to see what was going on and to hear what was said. A cat could hardly have squeezed through the closely packed legs of the crowd.

The rabbis from Jerusalem listened carefully to what Jesus said, but evidently they could find nothing wrong with his teaching. They may have said, "The Nazareth carpenter is a little too bold and a little too sure of himself. But what he says about the Law and the Prophets is good." Perhaps they wanted to give him some fatherly advice.

Suddenly an unexpected interruption caught the attention of everyone in the house. People in the street were the first to see what was going on. Four men had managed to haul up to the roof a man who was paralyzed by an illness. They pulled up the tiles and then pushed apart the small logs underneath until they could look right down into the room where Jesus was. "I don't mind if you hurt me. Get me down there," begged the sick man.

As soon as the men had made a hole big enough to squeeze the man through they lowered him into the room on a sheet.

Jesus had been bold in his teaching. Now he was equally bold in the use of the *power* in him. He turned to the paralyzed man and said kindly, "Take heart, son, your sins are forgiven."

No one in the room dared say anything to Jesus. Instead they whispered disapprovingly among themselves: "Who does he think he is? Only God can forgive sins."

Forgiveness is something that cannot be seen. Everyone knew that. To prove that the forgiveness was real, Jesus raised his voice in a ringing command: "Get up and go home!" And the paralyzed man did just that.

As the Gospel of Luke tells this story, Jesus used a new name for himself. He called himself the "Son of man." Literally, these words mean "a human being." But in Hebrew the word had another meaning which came from the Book of Daniel. There a figure called the "son of man" appears. He is the mysterious One whom God will send. Christians who read the Gospel of Luke would understand "Son of man" to mean the Promised One of God who will come in the last days of the world. The GOOD NEWS is that this "Son of man" came to conquer demons, to conquer sickness, and what is most marvelous of all, to conquer sin.

Did the people understand who Jesus was?

The Gospel of Mark says that the people were startled. They said, "We never saw anything like this!" They were impressed, and they liked Jesus. But they did not go so far as to believe that Jesus was really the Messiah of God.

18. The Sabbath Trap*

What is work?

This was an important question in Jesus' day. It was important because of the way the Sabbath commandment was interpreted. On that holy day a God-fearing person must do no work, yet there were many little things in daily life that were on the border line between work and nonwork.

The scribes approached this problem in a systematic way. They developed an analysis of work and came up with a list of exactly thirty-nine kinds of work. Each kind was interpreted in detail so that most questions about work and rest on a Sabbath could be answered.

Was healing a sick person on a Sabbath work? The scribes pondered that question and proposed what seemed to be a sensible answer. If it were a matter of life and death, healing would not be work. But if a man had a fever, for example, and it looked as if he would live to the next day, he should wait. To put cold, wet cloths on his head would be "work."

Jesus knew these Sabbath rules. He also knew that if he were very careful, no one could criticize him for violating the Sabbath. It was Jesus' custom to go to the synagogue every Sabbath as he had done since childhood. People approved. He had been a hard-working carpenter, obedient to the wishes of his parents, Joseph and Mary. People approved. He spoke gracious words as he explained the Law and the Prophets. People approved.

But Jesus did not care about being cautious and prudent. He was not worried about the approval of men. What he cared about supremely was doing the will of God.

Jesus had spoken boldly in the synagogue in Nazareth and had aroused bitter anger. This was not forgotten. All the freedom

* An account of Jesus healing a man with a withered hand on a Sabbath is given in Luke 6:6-11. Another account appears in Mark 3:1-6.

with which Jesus observed the Sabbath and taught his disciples
to do so, was not forgotten. The bigger the crowds around him,
the more suspicious the Pharisees became. They were convinced
that Jesus was a dangerous man.

One Sabbath in the synagogue Jesus looked at the row of
frowning Pharisees. He knew their thoughts. They were watching
him critically. They wanted an open-and-shut case to prove that
Jesus was a Sabbath-breaker. Breaking the Sabbath was a very
serious religious crime. Punishment at best was expulsion from
the Jewish people, the people of God. Actually, according to the
law the penalty for Sabbath-breaking was death.

Why did Jesus not act more cautiously? Why did he not do the
safe thing?

Above all, why did Jesus get *angry*?

The Gospel stories give a good clue. Jesus cared only about
the will of God. The will of God is to do good. This is more
important than all the "thou shalt not's" in the hundreds of Sabbath laws of the scribes and Pharisees. Jesus taught his followers
to look for what God willed for them first of all.

In the synagogue that day Jesus saw a man with a hand that
had never developed properly. Jesus asked him to hold out his
deformed hand. The man had always kept the withered little
wrist and fingers hidden under his robe so that people would not
notice. At Jesus' word he stretched it out obediently. And Jesus
healed it. How he did so, the Gospel writers do not describe.

When this happened the Pharisees got up and marched out of
the synagogue. They were indignant. The house of prayer had
been made a "house of work" and a place of "Sabbath-breaking."
Later on they got together with some politicians called Herodians
because they supported King Herod. Together they began to think
out a scheme against Jesus. They were not talking about how to
persuade Jesus that he was wrong. They were not talking about
expelling Jesus from the synagogue. They were talking about
"how to destroy him."

This was a grim business. A deadly danger hung over Jesus of Nazareth. On the one side were the large and curious crowds who dared him to do miracles. On the other side were religious experts who were plotting to find a way to have him killed.

19. Jesus' Most Popular Miracle*

The disciples felt worn out. Down at the lake there was so much coming and going of people that they did not even have time to eat. They felt the strain and wanted to get away where they could have peace and quiet, time to talk and to rest. Taking Jesus with them, they slipped away in a boat.

The men steered toward the hills east of Bethsaida. At the eastern and northern ends of the Sea of Galilee the hills rose up higher and higher into the blue distance. On the heights there were no towns, no farmsteads with vineyards on the slopes and plowed fields in the valleys. It was a barren region where the disciples could be alone with Jesus. The men had had an exciting and upsetting time preaching and healing in the villages to which Jesus had sent them. Up in the hills it would be cool and quiet.

Also there was a new danger to think about. The Herodians who had been in Capernaum had gone back to the palace of King Herod Antipas. No one could tell what might happen next because Herod was the king who had John the Baptist put to death.

The disciples could think of many stories that the Herodians could carry to the king. They might tell him about the little daughter of Jairus whom Jesus healed at the point of death while a crowd milled around outside, waiting for her funeral to begin. Or about a maniac in the mountain tombs who was strong enough to break chains but was now restored to health and meek as a

* Three accounts of the feeding of the multitude are Mark 6:30-44; 8:1-10; and John 6:1-14.

sheep. Or about lepers who were made clean and were now feasting with their wives and children. Or about Peter's mother-in-law
from whom Jesus had driven a fever and who had gone back to
her work in the kitchen.

What would the Herodians make of these stories?

It was well known that the king had become worried and
unsettled after he had done the awful deed of having John the
Baptist put to death. The king had been asking, "Who is this
Jesus?" One theory was that he was Elijah, the prophet, whom
everyone expected to return some Passover night shortly before
the Messiah would come. Others reckoned him to be a new
prophet. But Herod had his own theory. Hearing these stories
made him sure that Jesus was the ghost of John the Baptist.

The disciples had good reason to fear sly King Herod. But up
there in the hills, they would be safely out of the king's territory.

The plan of the disciples to cut across the lake and then dis-
appear into the hills did not work. Crowds spied the boat and went
in pursuit. They met Jesus on the shore and trailed along behind
him even when he left the last of the houses behind him.

Finally Jesus stopped in a pleasant bowl-shaped mountain valley. It was lush and green with the short-lived spring flowers that
followed the winter rains. Up there in the bright sun, the dusty
clothes of the people looked more shabby than ever. Jesus felt
sorry for them all—thin old men waiting to die, mothers worried
about their children, men who had left fields and shops to hear
about the things of God, and even the sick, gasping for breath
after the climb and hoping desperately for a cure. The ragged
crowd looked like "sheep without a shepherd."

Jesus stayed with the crowd and began to tell stories, one after
another. He talked kindly to the sick and healed them. The day
slipped away and the sun began to set beyond the western sea.

It was then that the worried disciples thought about supper.
Only Jesus was not worried. He took all the food that the disciples
could find—barley loaves and fishes from a boy who may have

carried them on a basket on his head. Perhaps the boy had been selling them in the crowd and this was all he had left; perhaps it was his own lunch.

Standing like a father at the evening meal, Jesus raised his hands to ask the blessing. Then he broke a barley loaf and gave the pieces to the disciples to carry to the rows and rows of people. Every time they came back, there was more to carry out.

The people ate gratefully, observing the Jewish custom of silence at mealtime. Then the disciples sat down to eat. Perhaps they were a little afraid of the dark bread which appeared so miraculously. But they need not have been uneasy. It was ordinary barley bread.

Each of the four Gospels tells this story. Matthew and Mark tell a second story which is almost identical to it. That makes six stories of this miracle in the Gospels. Among the early Christians this was the most popular miracle that Jesus performed. The story was told in every Christian church. As the early Christians told this story and looked back over the years, they learned to think about more than the bread that enters a person's body to build muscle and bone, brain and nerve. They saw in the multiplication of the loaves a sign of the kingdom of God. It was the good news that the Messiah of the kingdom had come. The bread he had to give was himself, the bread of life. Of that bread there is so much that it can satisfy the largest multitude. It will never fail.

20. The Greatest Miracle*

The Gospels tell many stories of miracles which Jesus did. We can read how Jesus changed water into wine at a wedding in Cana, how he commanded Peter to walk out on the water when

---

*John 3:1-21 is the story of Jesus and Nicodemus meeting at night. Nicodemus is also mentioned in John 7:50; 19:39.

he appeared at night on the Sea of Galilee, how he quieted a storm which threatened to swamp the little fishing boat, how he raised Lazarus from the tomb. The Gospels are full of *signs and wonders* of Jesus. A story of a miracle of Jesus is not simply an account of something that happened centuries ago, but a *sign*. A sign represents something. It points to something beyond itself. It points to a deeper meaning, to something that was astonishing and mysterious to the early Christians who gathered these stories and handed them down to us.

A person might think that Jesus' miracles were signs to persuade unbelieving people to believe in him. Yet Jesus never performed a miracle as if to say, "Now you have to believe in me. Just look at the miracles I can do!" Jesus had rejected that temptation when the Devil took him up on a high pinnacle and told him to leap off and float to the ground in front of the multitude. Indeed, Jesus became angry when people tried to make him perform a miracle to impress them and gain their faith. His own brothers wanted him to do that and he refused. Instead, every miracle Jesus did (with the possible exception of Matthew 21:18-19, which may not have been intended as a miracle) was a deed of love and pity. Jesus acted to help, not to amaze or impress people.

What kind of sign were Jesus' miracles? That question can be answered by looking at his greatest miracle. No one miracle which Jesus *did* was the greatest, whether it was restoring a person to health, or giving a blind man sight, or feeding all the people in a small town. Rather, it is near the beginning of the Gospel of John that we find the story of a man who experienced the greatest miracle. This man was a Pharisee named Nicodemus.

Nicodemus came to Jesus secretly in Jerusalem and talked with him far into the silent night—he and Jesus, alone. They talked about the mysteries of the kingdom of God and of how a person might "see" it. They talked about the unseen Spirit of God. They talked about the new beginning that every person who comes into God's kingdom must make. It is a new beginning like the birth of a person. The two men talked about the love and the judgment of God. They talked about faith and about eternal life.

"Can all this make sense?" Nicodemus thought.

"How can these things be?" he asked. He asked this even though he was a religious expert and a member of the Sanhedrin.

John's Gospel lets us see the wisest man of the Jews face to face with Jesus. Did Nicodemus understand? This passage in the Gospel of John gives no answer. It simply leaves Nicodemus and Jesus talking in the darkness of the night.

As we read the story, the questions of Nicodemus become our questions, and we listen more intently for an answer from Jesus. That is what the Gospel writer wanted to happen. He wrote so that we might meet Jesus and discover in his person the greatest miracle of all. The greatest miracle is the One who sat opposite Nicodemus in the darkness, beyond the yellow light of a lamp. The Gospel of John lets each Christian find out who that One is, and how in him a new life can begin. In him each believer can receive forgiveness of sins and life eternal.

Each miracle is a sign of the present power of the Lord, Jesus Christ. As a sign it points to God's greatest miracle in Christ himself.

IV

JESUS AND

HIS DISCIPLES

21. A Teacher Who Was Never Dull*

A GOOD TEACHER can make any subject interesting. Jesus was
that kind of teacher. He not only had the most important subject
in the world to teach; he was also the finest teacher the world has
known. Certainly the happiest times which the disciples spent
with Jesus were the hours when he was teaching.

The friendly twelve were the most faithful learners:
Simon Peter and his brother Andrew,
the younger sons of Zebedee, James and John,
Philip and Bartholomew (also called Nathanael),
Thomas and Levi (also called Matthew),
James, son of Alphaeus, and Simon the Canaanite,
Thaddaeus (also called Judas, son of James) and
Judas Iscariot.
Besides these twelve, there were many others who gathered around
Jesus.

Jesus taught in the manner of the teachers of his time. He liked to use stories and he was a skillful storyteller. He made everything he talked about sound lively and interesting. Often he used a kind of story called a parable. Old and young—no matter who were listening—liked the stories Jesus told. The parables Jesus told started people thinking because they usually had a hidden meaning.

Jesus' stories as we find them in the Gospels are very short and concise. They seem to have been condensed into a few brief notes. Originally, Jesus probably told these stories in a longer form in the manner of the storytellers of Oriental lands. Later on the stories were probably summed up in a shorter form in the Gospel traditions.

The stories Jesus told were not solemn, long-faced tales. Jesus told stories about two brothers fighting over inheriting their father's money, about a king who was planning a war, about a farmer who measured his barns for the harvest. Probably there was humor in his way of telling the stories, too. Jesus pictured a man who ran around with a slab of wood stuck in his eye, but who complained about a speck of dust in his neighbor's eye. He told about a man who got a camel down on its knees and then tried to squeeze the grumbling beast through the "needle's eye" (possibly a tiny gate in the city wall). Probably what was a joke to Oriental people in ancient times may not seem funny to us; our jokes would leave them just as baffled.

Of course, the main reason people crowded around Jesus was not that they wanted to be entertained. They came to hear and learn about a most important and exciting thing—the kingdom of God. What Jesus had to say was tremendously important because he could talk about the kingdom of God *from the inside.* He did not talk about what had been written about it in books,

* The collection of teachings of Jesus called the "Sermon on the Mount" is in Matthew 5—7.

but he talked about what he knew personally. He knew the kingdom; he was not guessing or supposing.

The great theme of Jesus' teaching was the kingdom of God,
but he did not stop to define it. Defining the kingdom was like
describing a great mountain. A mountain looks different from
various sides and at various times of the day, yet it is always the
same mountain. What Jesus had to say about the kingdom
sounded contradictory and surprising. His words were surprising
because he talked about the kingdom of God as something right
there around his listeners and in them. People had always thought
of the kingdom as something in the future; it was hard to see it
as already there. And what Jesus said seemed contradictory because he also talked about the kingdom as something that will
come in the future. At other times he simply described how people
in that kingdom live; people who "live in it" are those who live
under God's rule and obey him.

Jesus wanted to do more than just teach about the kingdom of
God. He had a beyond-the-horizon purpose for the chosen twelve.
They were not only to learn about the kingdom; they were also to
become apostles or ambassadors of the kingdom. What Jesus
taught, they were to teach. What he announced quietly to the
Twelve, they were to proclaim "from the housetops." Jesus
counted on these twelve men to carry on after him with the GOOD
NEWS of the kingdom of God.

Jesus explained this in a very colorful way. As the young men
looked at him with bright, eager eyes, he said, "You are salt . . .
salt of the earth." As any fisherman knows, fish spoil quickly and
there is hardly anything that has a more offensive odor than
rotting fish. However, if fish are put in a brine made of salt and
water, they will keep for months. Perhaps Jesus meant that the
disciples should serve as a kind of preservative in a world that
would otherwise change from bad to worse somewhat like rotting
fish. Or Jesus may simply have meant that the twelve disciples
should be like a pinch of salt. A little salt goes a long way; with-

out it food is tasteless and unappetizing. So, although they were only twelve men, what they were to do and say would reach out into all the world like a pinch of salt in food.

Again, Jesus declared, "You are a light . . . light of the world." At night no one covers the one lamp in a farmhouse or lets the expensive oil burn to no purpose. Rather, the lamp is placed where it will light the whole room. The little lamp sheds its light far into the darkness. In a similar way Jesus' disciples were to become a light for the whole world.

Jesus talked about "salt" and "light," but he did not spend a long time explaining what he meant. This made the way Jesus taught fascinating. Jesus let his disciples puzzle out for themselves what he meant. He talked about salt and light and let the disciples figure out a hidden meaning. In later years the early Christians discovered how true and powerful the words of Jesus were. The light of the GOOD NEWS did shine far, far enough to reach from one end of the Roman Empire to the other.

There were times when the disciples could not understand what Jesus meant. They heard and remembered, but did not comprehend. They always found him interesting but often puzzling, fascinating and yet unsettling, plain to understand and yet mysterious, easy to listen to but hard to forget. Sometimes they asked him questions as if he were a close friend; at other times they were afraid to speak out because they realized that their teacher was more than an ordinary man.

What and how did this teacher teach? The Gospel of Matthew makes use of a famous collection of the sayings of Jesus, the teacher. After the Gospel was written, this collection became known as the "Sermon on the Mount" although the collection is neither a sermon as the word is used today nor was it spoken at one time and place. The Sermon on the Mount is a fine sampling of what Jesus talked about as a teacher. It begins with a poem of eight Beatitudes and closes with the Parable of the Two Builders.

22. The Happy People of the Kingdom*

From the rocky slope of a high hill the disciples could look down on the main road below. A caravan was moving past. First came a long line of fine horsemen. This was the bodyguard. After them three enclosed vans appeared. They were slung on poles and carried by stalwart slaves. The brightly colored curtains of the vans were drawn shut against the sun, and the curious disciples could not see who was inside. Other servants followed with pack animals and traveling wagons. As the young fishermen watched each bit of that colorful procession of a rich man's caravan pass by, they may have talked about how many servants he had, or how much it would cost to buy one of his horses, or from what far-off city he had come.

"That man has a fine life. He doesn't have to worry about where his next meal is coming from. He has more money than he can spend. They'll give him the best when he gets to Capernaum tonight."

To these Galilean peasants, the rich foreigner who passed by seemed to command every luxury and pleasure in the world. How could they help but envy him!

But when Jesus began to speak, he turned all their ideas upside down. He spoke about the happy people in the kingdom of God. He spoke in a way that meant, "You are those happy people of the kingdom!"

With a sweep of his hand Jesus seemed to gather the disciples into the kingdom. Beyond them, it would include the early Christians who gave their testimony of faith in the four Gospels. All who love and obey God would be the people of the kingdom. God's kingdom comes to all who love and trust in Jesus, to those to whom is given faith to find in the person of Jesus the will and love of God.

* The Beatitudes can be found in Matthew 5:3-12 and Luke 6:20-26.

What Jesus said about the happy people of the kingdom is summed up in sayings called the Beatitudes—

Blessed are the poor . . .

Blessed are those who mourn . . .

Blessed are the merciful . . .

Blessed are those who are persecuted . . .

Each Beatitude is a surprise. Each is a puzzling contradiction. The poor will own the kingdom; the mourners are to be congratulated and called happy; the meek will claim the whole world; the merciful have great happiness awaiting them; the persecuted will rejoice. This is the way it will be in the kingdom of God because this is God's kingdom and he acts in surprising ways.

Jesus did not stop to explain in detail what he meant, but what he said the disciples could never forget. They remembered these eight Beatitudes in the years that followed. And the deeper meanings of the Beatitudes became plain to them as they gave their lives in serving Jesus Christ. They discovered that the only real way to understand Jesus is to love and obey him.

Each Beatitude has a key word that describes a person of the kingdom as he is right now. Understanding the key word is a help toward uncovering the surprising meaning Jesus gave to that Beatitude. As the disciples remembered the Beatitudes, they learned that the surprising things Jesus said were true.

The key word in the first Beatitude is *poor*. A poor person is usually a humble person. He has no fine clothes to make him seem important or to make him proud and vain. He has no bags of gold; nor does he have the power and respect that money brings. The poor persons whom Jesus calls "happy" are the *poor in spirit*. They are humble-minded people who trust in God completely. Because they seem powerless when compared with the high and mighty in this world, they are often oppressed and mistreated. When the world oppresses them, they trust in the power of God. Jesus is saying, "How blessed are you who feel your need of God, for to you his kingdom belongs!"

When the Christian church began, Mary Magdalene was not a rich or an important person. She was not a respected woman, either. Yet because of her trust and faith in Jesus she became one of the happy people of the kingdom.

A key word in another Beatitude is *mourn*. A person who mourns is a person who feels the suffering and grief of others. He mourns because he loves others so much; he has sympathy for the grief of others. To be truly happy in God's eyes is to be able to love so much that you become painfully sensitive to what is evil and wrong in the world and in yourself. The opposite of a person who mourns is a person who simply doesn't care, who never feels sorry. Such a person may seem gay and full of laughter, but he is not really happy in God's sight. In this Beatitude Jesus promises that this mourning, this grief, will not last long. He is saying, "How blessed are you who mourn, for you have the promise that the tears which you shed will be turned to joy through the comfort that comes from God's Messiah!"

Jesus told a parable about a publican who went to the temple to pray. He was a person who mourns. He beat his breast in grief; he felt the heavy weight of his sins and guilt upon him; he cried out: "God be merciful to me a sinner." He was truly downcast and wretched—yet he was, in the eyes of Jesus, one of the truly happy people of the kingdom!

What the word *meek* means was clear to the disciples. They had grown up in the country and they knew farm life. They had been to the marketplace where oxen and horses were sold. The owner would praise a pair of oxen by saying, "You won't find a more meek team in all of Galilee." A meek horse or ox was an animal that was strong and obedient to its master. Such an animal was useful because it was well trained.

A meek person does not strut around as if he owned the world; his strength is in obeying God who created the world. A meek person is not weak or timid. He is strong because he depends upon God who truly rules the world. Jesus is saying, "How happy are those who claim nothing for themselves, for everything is theirs through God in whom they trust!"

In the early Christian church there was a young man named Timothy. He was put in charge of the church at Ephesus when Paul left. Sometimes he felt shy and self-conscious. Yet he became a strong man because he obeyed fully the call to serve God. This made him a happy person of the kingdom.

It sometimes seems that the person who gets ahead in the world is one who is aggressive, bold, and hard. Not so in the kingdom which Jesus proclaimed. Rather, it is the *merciful* person who is truly happy. A merciful person is a person who forgives. The opposite is a person who holds a grudge, who is always trying to get even. Such a person is on the way to becoming the most miserable person in the world. "You are happy if you care about people," Jesus promises, "for God himself is merciful. How blessed are you who show mercy to other persons, for you live under the forgiveness of God. He will show mercy to you on the Day of Judgment."

When Paul was in prison in Philippi, the jailer ordered that he be beaten. All the rough, cruel treatment which Paul endured in prison he could blame on the jailer. Yet he did not yield to thoughts of hatred or revenge. In that way he was one of the really happy people of the kingdom.

The *persecuted* have much to suffer. Jesus promised no easy life to his disciples. He prepared them for a rough time. They would be driven out of the synagogues. They would be beaten and stoned. They would be caged up in prison, or they might be fed to the lions. The reason for the persecution of the early Christians was that they refused to give up their faith. They trusted completely in God. People who trust in God are truly happy. People who belong to Jesus and who live in God's kingdom can expect to be persecuted.

Outwardly, the situation of the early Christians seemed to be a miserable one. Yet in time of persecution they found even greater joy in their faith in God. Jesus is saying, "How blessed are you who are persecuted for my sake, for your suffering will be turned into joy everlasting."

An angry mob hurled stones at Stephen, the first Christian martyr. They cursed him as a blasphemer. Yet in his dying hour, Stephen prayed for his persecutors. We can be sure that in the painful triumph of his death he was one of the happy people of the kingdom.

23. Radical Righteousness*

The people of Jesus' day had a yardstick by which they measured any teacher of the things of God. That yardstick was the "Law of Moses." The question in people's minds as they listened to Jesus was, "What does this new teacher say about the Law?" In Jesus' day, religious teachers spent most of their time studying and explaining the laws of Moses. They trusted in the Law to show men how to earn salvation. They believed that God blessed those who kept the Law and punished those who broke it. They believed that a person could earn his way into God's kingdom by obeying God's laws perfectly.

Jesus knew that the same kind of question was in the minds of his disciples: "Do you accept the Law of Moses?" Jesus answered that question with both a "yes" and a "no." In the first place he assured his followers that he had no intention of destroying the Law. He came to fulfill the Law. Not even the dotting on an "i" in the Law would be changed. Jesus came to fulfill the Law in himself. That was Jesus' "yes" to the Law.

Jesus, however, did not think of the Law as simply a collection of rules, written down in a book. Rather, the Law is a guide to the

* The six examples of radical righteousness in the Sermon on the Mount are in Matthew 5:17-48.

will of God. Jesus poured out his life's energy to seek and obey that will of God. He came to reveal the deeper meaning of God's will. And in that sense he spoke a "no" to the Law because he showed that the Law—all the rules and regulations—was not enough.

One kind of righteousness is a righteousness that comes by obeying each rule, each "thou shalt not," in the laws of Moses. Jesus was not satisfied with that righteousness. A person might obey many rules and yet not obey the *full* will of God. That is why Jesus spoke of another kind of righteousness. We may call it the radical righteousness of the kingdom.

"Radical" means to go to the root of anything. Radical righteousness goes to the root of God's will for us. It goes beyond all the dozens of "thou shalt not's" of the Law.

The surprising thing about this radical righteousness is that it does not add more rules, regulations, precepts, or commands to the Law. Instead, it cuts through to the heart of God's will for us. That will, as Jesus explained it, is the "law" of love.

In the Sermon on the Mount we can find six examples of the radical righteousness of the kingdom of God. No doubt, Jesus gave many more examples. These six are enough to help us see the deeper meaning of the "law" of love.

Each example Jesus gave of the radical righteousness of the kingdom helps us see that this righteousness is not a new set of laws to be obeyed. These six examples simply show how love acts under certain conditions. Jesus did not come to give his disciples more laws to obey so that God would accept them into the kingdom. A person cannot earn his way into the kingdom. To be in that kingdom is a gift God gives to a person. The six examples of radical righteousness help us see what kind of life a person lives when God has called him through his Son to be in his kingdom.

One of these six examples is the law "Do not murder." Jesus used this example to contrast the two kinds of righteousness. The first kind was the normal interpretation of this law of Moses.

People understood it to mean that all they had to do was avoid killing anybody. "That's easy enough," said the disciples. They had no intention to do murder. Jesus knew their thoughts. His eyes flashed. He knew that a person can take this law and make it into something that hides rather than reveals God's will. He looked for the deeper will of God, for the radical righteousness.

Jesus was bold and dramatic. He clearly declared that to hate a person is as wrong in God's eyes as to kill him. Radical righteousness applies to our feelings and thoughts as well as to our deeds. The will of God in the law "Do not murder" pierces deep into our thoughts, our feelings, our attitudes to other people. Jesus leads us to a deeper meaning of the "law" of love.

People shook their heads. Such teaching made them feel very uncomfortable. Who could say, "I've never hated anybody," or "I've never carried a grudge"?

The last two examples of radical righteousness in the Sermon on the Mount are the most surprising and puzzling of all. One tells what Jesus said about the law of revenge. The other tells what he said about the Old Testament law of love.

The law of revenge was summed up in the words "An eye for an eye and a tooth for a tooth." Originally, that meant that if someone knocked out one of your teeth, you were entitled to equal compensation—not unlimited revenge, such as knocking out a whole mouthful of teeth. Jesus, however, rejected all hatred and all "getting even." It is not God's will that we should seek revenge:

> *But I say unto you, Do not resist one who is evil.*
> *But if any one strikes you on the right cheek,*
> *turn to him the other also. . . .*

Jesus looked deep into the heart of God. God's will is the way of love, not of hate.

Again Jesus' hearers must have felt uncomfortable. This seemed very difficult. It seemed impractical. Yet Christians who have tried this way of love, of nonviolent resistance to evil, declare that it takes more courage to love than to hate. They have found that the power of love is stronger than the power of hate. Hate divides people and turns them against each other. Love unites, heals, and strengthens. They have learned what God's love means in Jesus' death upon the cross for us. Jesus chose these unforgettable sayings to help us see that God's will for us is to show love to all people. It is a love that liberates us from hatred, grudge-bearing, egotism, and revenge.

The last example, the law of love, meant in Old Testament times that it was the duty of each Jew to love his own countrymen and to hate the Gentiles. This law divided the world into two parts: friends (neighbors) and enemies (outsiders). Jesus declared in unmistakable terms that to God there are no outsiders. God loves all people perfectly, that is, completely. He "sends rain on the just and on the unjust."

> *But I say to you, Love your enemies*
> *and pray for those who persecute you. . . .*
> *You, therefore, must be perfect,*
> *as your heavenly Father is perfect.*

The time was to come when the disciples would see Jesus nailed to a cross. Then, when he was surrounded by his enemies, he prayed, "Father, forgive them, for they know not what they do." Jesus did not turn in hatred against anyone. The love of which he speaks is not simply a soft, kindly feeling such as you might have when someone gives you a wonderful present. Rather, it is the kind of love that God showed for all mankind when he sent Jesus into the world.

A citizen of the kingdom is one who learns to have this kind of love and concern for all people. This is the radical righteousness of the kingdom.

In the Sermon on the Mount sayings Jesus gave his disciples a glimpse of the radical righteousness of the kingdom in a way they could not forget. These sayings open the doors to discovering many other ways in which the "law" of love guides the Christian.

24. How Kingdom People Pray*

The disciples saw how often Jesus looked for a quiet place to pray. Sometimes he got up very early in the morning and looked for a place where he could be alone in prayer. They saw that prayer was very important to Jesus. So the disciples begged Jesus to teach them how to pray. They wanted to be able to pray as Jesus did. John the Baptist had taught his disciples certain prayers; Jesus' disciples expected him to do the same for them.

As usual, Jesus was a surprising teacher. He taught the disciples a prayer and he taught them how to pray. In the Sermon on the Mount he warned the disciples against long, showy prayers. A prayer is not better because it is long. God knows what we ask even before we put our prayer into words. Prayer should never be used to show off, as persons in Jesus' day did when they offered long, impressive prayers in public and were admired by the people in the marketplace or synagogue. This was a misuse of prayer. The prayers of Jesus as they are given in the Gospels are extremely short and to the point.

Jesus taught his followers never to hesitate to pray. He promised:

Ask, and it will be given you;
seek, and you will find;
knock, and it will be opened to you.

What a prayer should be like and how kingdom people pray becomes clear in a model prayer Jesus taught his disciples. It came to be known as the Lord's Prayer. Like the other sayings of Jesus, this prayer looks deeply into the heart and will of God. It is a prayer which does not try to tell God what to do but trusts in him completely. It is a prayer of faith. If you really pray (not

---

* The Lord's Prayer appears in Matthew 6:9-13 and Luke 11:1-4. Other important sayings of Jesus about prayer are in Matthew 6:5-8, 14-15; 7:7-12.

just say) the Lord's Prayer, you must put yourself entirely at God's disposal. This was what Jesus did. This is what he asks his followers to do.

Like the Beatitudes, the Lord's Prayer is in the form of a Hebrew poem or psalm. It has two verses, each containing five lines. The first is a "thy" verse and the second is an "us" verse. As Jesus himself had always done, he expects his disciples to ask first: "What is God's will?" That is why the prayer begins with three "thy" petitions: *thy name, thy kingdom, thy will.* Jesus trusted completely that God will establish his kingdom:

> *Our Father who art in heaven,*
> *Hallowed be thy name.*
> *Thy kingdom come,*
> *Thy will be done,*
>   *On earth as it is in heaven.*

This is a family prayer, a prayer for the people of the family of God. Nowhere in this model prayer did Jesus tell his disciples to pray for themselves alone. The people of the kingdom of God belong to a great family. All are gathered together in the first two words of the prayer, *Our Father.*

"Seek first God's kingdom and his righteousness," Jesus taught his disciples. "Blessed are the poor in spirit," he told them. The spirit of these sayings is reflected in this prayer. It puts God and his kingdom in first place. It expresses humble and complete trust in what God will do.

The five lines of the first verse are a description of the way Jesus lived. He honored God in all he did and said. The GOOD NEWS which he brought was the GOOD NEWS of the kingdom of God. The life and deeds of Jesus are a foretaste of the kingdom of God. In Jesus that kingdom came into the world in a hidden way. Jesus taught that in the future, at a time known only to God, the kingdom will come outwardly in all its glory and power. That will be when Jesus Christ comes again at the end of the world.

In the second verse, the Lord's Prayer turns to the things that people worried about most. "Do not be anxious about your life," Jesus said, "what you shall eat or what you shall drink, nor about your body, what you shall put on." In a land where many went hungry, Jesus taught his disciples to pray for "daily bread." By "bread" Jesus meant not only the barley loaves people ate every day. He also meant all that is necessary for life and health, such as clothes, shelter, trustworthy friends, peace, and so on. God gives us these things all the time. In this prayer Jesus taught his followers to praise and thank God for what he gives and to trust that he will continue to provide for us.

> *Give us this day our daily bread;*
> *And forgive us our debts*
>   *As we also have forgiven our debtors;*
> *And lead us not into temptation,*
>   *But deliver us from evil.*

The body hungers for food and the spirit seeks forgiveness. For both we turn to God. We need forgiveness because of our "debts" to God. We owe these debts because of our sinfulness. A person in the kingdom of God learns to know God's forgiveness and to forgive others in turn. The opposite is also true: a person who does not forgive cannot be open to receive the forgiveness of God. Receiving God's forgiveness and showing forgiveness cannot be separated.

"From evil" may also mean "from the Evil One." If so, Jesus' model prayer closes with a petition for protection against Satan. Satan seeks to lure the people of the kingdom away from complete trust in God. This temptation comes to all of God's children. Even Jesus was tempted. Jesus, who triumphed over Satan, taught his followers to pray that God would guard and keep them against "the Evil One" and his temptations. Centuries later, after the Gospels were written, Christians added a doxology to the Lord's Prayer.

25. Two Gates . . . Two Trees . . . Two Builders*

Jesus was an interesting teacher in the way he made his meaning vivid and clear. He used word pictures of common things that everyone knew. People could easily remember what Jesus said because of the bold, dramatic way he taught. In the Sermon on the Mount there are three striking pairs of pictures—two gates, two trees, two builders.

The people of Jesus' day often compared the religious life to a journey. In that journey the important thing is to pick the right road. One road leads to life; the other road leads to death.

Jesus, also, spoke of the road that leads to eternal life with God, and he spoke of the gateway through which a person must enter. One gate is small and narrow; the road to it is a difficult one. Only a few choose this road and enter through the little gate. But the other gate is wide, and the road is easy. Many travel that road. It is the narrow gate, however, that leads to eternal life. Jesus said, "Enter by the narrow gate. . . ."

When Christians were few and life for them was hard, they liked to remember this saying of Jesus because they had found it to be true. Only a few chose the narrow gate. Jesus called his followers to a hard life, but the road leads to life eternal.

Jesus knew that the time would come when his followers would have to decide how to tell a true teacher from a false one. There would be many teachers; each would claim that his teaching was true. Jesus said that a teacher of the things of God is like a tree. It is easy to tell a useful tree from a useless one. All one has to do is to look at what the tree produces. No one expects to pick grapes from a thorny shrub or harvest figs from a thistle bush.

The disciples and the early Christians learned what Jesus meant. A true teacher shows by the life he lives whether what

* The sayings of the two gates, the two trees, and the two builders are in Matthew 7:13-27.

BEWARE OF FALSE PROPHETS, WHO COME TO YOU
IN SHEEP'S CLOTHING
BUT INWARDLY ARE RAVENOUS WOLVES.
YOU WILL KNOW THEM BY THEIR FRUITS.
ARE GRAPES GATHERED
FROM THORNS,
OR FIGS FROM THISTLES?

he teaches is good or evil, true or false. When false teachers came, the early Christians remembered this saying of Jesus about the two trees—the tree that bears good fruit and the tree that does not.

The Sermon on the Mount closes with the vivid Parable of the Two Builders. To understand this parable we need to remember that Palestine is a dry country. During much of the year it does not rain at all; it may not rain very much for several years. A person can build a house and live in it for a long time before a storm comes. But when the rain does come, it may be a cloudburst, filling empty stream beds. The water rushes and tumbles down in a mighty stream, and the wind howls around the house. The swirling water will sweep away anything that is not built on a strong foundation. A good builder will build his house on bedrock. A careless one may build on sand, and the storm will sweep it away.

A person who hears the sayings of Jesus and responds to him in faith is like the wise builder. He will stand firm against the storms of life.

The Sermon on the Mount describes a new life. It is a hard and different life, but it is the life God expects us to live in his kingdom. It is not man's way of living, but it is the life of the citizens of God's kingdom. The kind of life Jesus put before his disciples is one that they could not live by their own strength. Each part of the Sermon on the Mount helps the believer to see how different his life is from the kind of life Jesus expected him to live. A Christian's response to the Sermon should be a confession of his own sinfulness, a prayer for forgiveness, and a cry for strength to do the will of his Lord more completely.

Christians can be sure of this help because of the man who spoke the words of the Sermon on the Mount. He is Jesus, our Savior.

V

PARABLES OF

THE KINGDOM

26. He Said to Them, "Listen!"*

THE PEOPLE CROWDED AROUND JESUS so closely that only those near him could see and hear. Others who were unable to elbow their way through the crowd could hear only snatches of what Jesus was saying. Jesus saw what was happening so he got into a boat at the water's edge. After the commotion of this change was over and the crowd was seated on the shore so that all could see and hear, Jesus began speaking. The water acted like a sounding board. "LISTEN!" he cried.

People stopped talking. All eyes were directed to the man in the boat.

"LISTEN!"

People bent forward to hear. They knew that more than hearing was needed. They must pay attention. They must look for a special meaning in Jesus' words. Hidden in what the great Teacher had to say was something special each must find for himself.

"LISTEN! A sower went out to sow . . ."

People liked the way Jesus began. He did not speak in a dull, stuffy way. He began with no solemn exhortation. Instead he started immediately to tell a story. In Oriental lands the skill of a storyteller has long been appreciated and respected. In modern times you can see the storyteller in the streets of the Arab side of Jerusalem. When he starts a story, a crowd gathers.

The kind of story Jesus often told is called a parable. There are many parables in later Jewish literature and there are some parables in the Old Testament. But no one has ever matched the skill which Jesus displayed in telling parables. Jesus often began by saying, "With what can we compare the kingdom of God, or what parable shall we use for it?"

We may imagine Jesus looking at the crowd. There sat a farmer, his wife, and his sons. A traveling merchant stopped on the road to listen. Children wriggled on their mothers' laps. A few boys stopped skipping stones across the lake to listen. They all liked Jesus' stories. They were stories about things the people knew and had seen themselves. They were stories that delighted a person accustomed to think in a Hebrew way because each story concealed a special meaning.

What was peculiar about this Hebrew way of thinking? Why did the Jewish people enjoy a story with a double meaning? We may trace this Hebrew way of thinking in the forms of writing often used in the Old Testament. One is the *proverb*. A large book of the Old Testament, the Book of Proverbs, is filled with many wise sayings. Jesus himself used proverbs. One that he quoted in

---

* Matthew 13 and 21 are two chapters famous for parables of Jesus. Parables in the Old Testament include the Parable of the Rich and Poor, 2 Samuel 12:1-4; The Thistle and the Cedar, 2 Kings 14:9; the Plowman, Isaiah 28:23-29. Prophets sometimes acted out parables, as did Jeremiah. See Jeremiah 13:1-7; 19:1-2, 10. The way the apostle Paul wrote about the body and its members may be regarded as a kind of parable. See 1 Corinthians 12:12-27.

the synagogue in Nazareth was short and to the point: "Physician, heal thyself." This proverb, like many others, has the kernel of a story in it. This proverb suggests a story about a doctor who claimed that he could heal the sick. But when he got sick he was unable to heal himself. People then said, "If he's a good doctor, he should be able to heal himself." This was shortened to the proverb "Physician, heal thyself." The proverb compares (a) what the physician said with (b) what he did, or could not do.

The Hebrews enjoyed making comparisons. Hebrew poetry is full of all kinds of comparisons. Jesus was familiar with psalm verses such as "He is like a tree planted by streams of water, that yields its fruit in its season, and its leaf does not wither." The famous psalm verse "The Lord is my shepherd, I shall not want" compares God to a protecting shepherd. A great hymn of the church, based on Psalm 46, uses this Hebrew form of poetry: "A mighty fortress is our God, A bulwark never failing."

Hebrew proverbs and poetry made use of comparisons. From these it was just a step to the Hebrew parable. A parable is a kind of parallel story. It explains something that is unknown by describing something like it that people already know. For example, Jesus told a parable about a mustard seed. A mustard seed is about the size of the head of a pin. It looks like a radish seed. In Palestine the plant grows rapidly to become a surprisingly large bush in which a bird can easily take shelter. Everyone knew about mustard seeds and the size of the plant. That was the known side of the parable. The unknown in this parable was the kingdom of God. Jesus said that the kingdom of God is like a mustard seed. There he stopped. He did not explain why this is so. He wanted his hearers to find out for themselves what the hidden meaning was. For that reason the Hebrews called a parable a "dark saying" or a "riddle." People in Jesus' day delighted in riddles just as people today enjoy crossword puzzles.

Most of Jesus' parables are riddles about the kingdom of God. Each riddle is told in story form. People could easily remember the story. Then they had to puzzle out the meaning themselves because Jesus seldom explained his parables. Only in two cases do the Gospels record an explanation which Jesus gave. Jesus explained the Parable of the Sower and the Parable of the Tares.

The early Christians looked for hidden meanings in the parable of the mustard seed. Christians knew from experience that the beginnings of the church were very small. They were like a tiny seed. But the GOOD NEWS of the kingdom spread swiftly. Then, like the birds of the parable, many people came to find shelter in it. Many people came to faith in Jesus Christ.

27. The Sower*

In Jesus' day a farmer's fields were small. All the work was done by hand. First came the planting, then the plowing. The farmer carried his seed grain in a pouch slung along over his shoulder. With each stride across the field he would scatter a handful of grain. Naturally, he could not limit his sowing to the good ground only. Some of the kernels were bound to fall on the hard-trodden paths across the stubble field. Some rolled among outcroppings of boulders where the soil was shallow. Some fell into nooks among the rocks where only thorns and thistles grew.

Then came the plowing. With a homemade wooden plow, drawn by two oxen, the farmer loosened the soil, turned it over, and covered the seed that he had scattered.

Every farmer knew what would happen next. If the winter rains came at the right time, the grain would sprout. Earliest to germinate would be the seed in the shallow soil which was warmed by the rock beneath. Soon these new stalks would turn yellow because the ground would dry out quickly and the plants could not

---

* The Parable of the Sower, also called the Parable of the Four Kinds of Soil, is in Mark 4:1-20.

send down deep roots. The seed among the thorns would also
come up, but the weeds would grow faster and choke it out. The
seed that dropped on the paths would never take root because
birds would eat it up. But the seed on good soil would develop
heavy heads of grain. Jesus spoke of a harvest a hundred times the
amount of seed planted—a bumper crop. If a farmer planted
half a bushel of seed to an acre, he would reap a crop of fifty
bushels an acre.

The disciples could not figure out the meaning of this parable.
It was like a riddle they could not solve. Finally they asked Jesus
for an explanation. Jesus explained that he was comparing the
seed of the farmer to the Word—the GOOD NEWS of the kingdom
of God. Jesus was spreading that news generously. He knew that
many who were listening to him would forget, or would become
busy with other things, or would even turn against him. But in
some the GOOD NEWS would take deep root and bear results in a
Christian life. As disciples, the followers of Jesus were to be
sowers of the GOOD NEWS everywhere. In some places it would be
received by willing hearts who would bring forth fruit in their
lives in a harvest of faith.

When Christians became discouraged, they remembered this
parable. They went ahead, like the sower, spreading God's Word
far and wide, even though many who heard did not accept it and
seemed cold-hearted.

28. Buried Treasure*

Many a battle had been fought on the Plain of Esdraelon,
which cuts across Galilee. When foreign armies marched across
the plain the people of the villages buried their valuables and fled

* The Parable of the Hidden Treasure and others like it are in Matthew 13:44-52.

into the hills. When the soldiers had gone, they came back to dig up their valuables again. Sometimes, however, the owners did not come back but were carried away into slavery or killed in the fighting. So there was much secret treasure hidden in the earth. In 1950, archaeologists dug in the ruins of Qumran near the Dead Sea. They found a jar crammed full of silver coins. It was buried treasure that had never been claimed. These coins have been polished and are now on exhibit in a museum at Jerusalem, spilling out in a shining heap from the mouth of a brown earthenware jar.

It was the law in Jesus' day that whoever found buried treasure in his land had the right to keep it. If he owned the land, he owned what was under it. Many a poor farmer lived in the hope of some day finding secret treasure.

Jesus told a story about a man who found buried treasure in a field he did not own. He did what almost anyone listening to Jesus would have done. Quickly he covered up the treasure. Then he schemed how he could buy that field. He sold all he owned and by one pretext or other, made a bargain with the owner to buy the field. All the while he kept his secret. When the field was finally his, he hurried to get the treasure buried in the ground and make it his own.

The kingdom of heaven is like that treasure, said Jesus. He did not need to explain. The kingdom is worth all that a man may possess. Jesus asked his disciples, "Have you understood all this?" The disciples said, "Yes."

A parable leads from the familiar to the less familiar. It is a story about earthly things with a heavenly meaning. It was up to each follower of Jesus to discover for himself the meaning hidden in what Jesus said. The stories Jesus told may seem simple, but each one has a special meaning for the kingdom of God.

In this story we can hear Jesus asking us, "Are you looking for the real treasure?"

29. Who Is My Neighbor?*

Some parables are scattered through the Gospels like pearls that have dropped off a string. We cannot know when or where Jesus told each parable. Other parables are part of a longer story. We are told how Jesus came to tell such parables and to whom he told them. For example, one day an expert in the Law of Moses (called a lawyer) came to Jesus. He had a problem which was good for a whole afternoon of discussion and argument. His lead-off question was: "What shall I do to inherit eternal life?"

Actually, the Law-of-Moses expert was not looking for help, or guidance, or information. He wanted to trap Jesus. He wanted to involve Jesus in a legal argument in such a way that Jesus would look foolish.

"You're a lawyer," Jesus replied. "Surely you know the Law. What does it say?"

The man quoted the Old Testament: "You shall love the Lord your God with all your heart, and with all your soul, and with all your strength, and with all your mind; and your neighbor as yourself." The lawyer knew the words perfectly. He was perfectly sure of himself.

Jesus knew that if the man would ever really try to put these words into deeds, he would soon discover how helpless he was. He would discover how hard it is to love God with all one's heart. Then, perhaps, he would lose his pride and would turn to God for forgiveness and help. He might become one of those who are "poor in spirit." Then the kingdom would come to him. That may be why Jesus said to the lawyer: "Do that—love your God and your neighbor completely—and you will live."

At that the man grew a little angry. He had meant to keep control of the argument and lead Jesus on. Instead, Jesus was leading him on in a way he had not expected. He had wanted to

* The Parable of the Good Samaritan is in Luke 10:25-37.

make Jesus look foolish; now he was feeling foolish himself. The lawyer tried to wriggle out of his uncomfortable position. He wanted to get something to argue about, so he asked, "But who *is* my neighbor?"

This, thought the lawyer, would lead into a discussion. Perhaps he thought that few people were fit to be his neighbors—not the Gentiles, not the tax collectors, not the common people who did not know the Law as well as he did, not the sinners who did not keep the Law.

Again Jesus turned the tables on the lawyer. He did so by telling him the Parable of the Good Samaritan. This parable is not really an answer to the lawyer's question "Who is my neighbor?" Instead, Jesus raised a more important question: "To whom are you a neighbor?" The lawyer had asked, "Who deserves my love and help? Who is good enough to be my neighbor?" Jesus asked the lawyer another question instead, "Who needs your love and help?"

At the end of the story of the Good Samaritan Jesus asked the lawyer, "Which of the three—the priest, the Levite, the Samaritan—do you think proved neighbor to the man who fell among the thieves?"

The lawyer blushed. He got the point. In a low voice he began his answer. He looked at the ground to avoid the piercing gaze of Jesus. "The one who showed mercy on him," he mumbled.

Jesus then said, "Go and do likewise."

Jesus remained master of the situation. That is the way it is when we encounter him.

The disciples also understood. The Samaritan helped the beaten and robbed man, not because he wanted to earn God's favor, but because the man needed help. Trying to be like the Samaritan will not bring anyone into the kingdom, but those who *are* in the kingdom do love their neighbors. In the world, people care about themselves. In the kingdom, a believer cares about anyone who needs help.

30. The Free-Spending Brother*

One of the longest parables in the Gospels is a story of two brothers. The brother who gets the most attention in this parable is the younger one. He was very different from his older brother. The older brother was obedient and hardworking; the younger brother wanted only to enjoy himself. In the village the people spoke highly of the dutiful older brother, but there was probably a lot of gossip about the lighthearted younger brother.

The two brothers expected to inherit the property of their old father. According to Jewish law, the firstborn son would get a double share. The younger brother knew this. He had calculated just how much his one-third share would be. He took advantage of his father's kindness and demanded his share of the inheritance immediately. The father gave in to his son's wishes. The fun-loving boy immediately took the money and went off to a distant country where he spent it in loose living.

A famine came and the money was soon used up. The younger son was reduced to tending pigs. (To the Jews, pigs were unclean; tending hogs was about as low as a man could get.) So great was the famine that the starving young man even envied the pigs for their fodder, the coarse pods of the carob tree.

All the while, the older brother did his work on his father's estate conscientiously. He was a model son.

Then the free-spending brother "came to himself." He knew that he had done wrong, but now he was at the end of his rope. He had spent his inheritance foolishly. This was regarded by the Jews as one of the most shameful things a man could do. It was a man's highest duty to hold on to inherited property and to keep it in the family. More than this, the ragged young man sitting among the grunting pigs realized that he had sinned against God. Mentally he rehearsed the confession he would make: "Father, I

* The Parable of the Prodigal Son is in Luke 15:11-32.

have sinned against heaven and before you; I am no longer worthy to be called your son; treat me as one of your hired servants." Over and over he pictured what he would do when he came home.

The way the free-spending youth pictured his homecoming was very different from what actually happened. He had not understood how deeply his father loved him. He had taken too lightly the fact that he was a son of his father. Even before he reached the house, his father ran out to meet him. As the son tried to pour out his confession, the father poured out his love.

"Give him the best robe!" This was normally reserved for distinguished guests.

"Give him a ring." A ring was a symbol of importance and dignity. It made the boy a son again.

"Get sandals for the young man!" Sandals were the sign of a free man and not a slave.

"Prepare the fatted calf!" The fatted calf was reserved for the greatest festival of the year.

This was all too much for the faithful older brother. He boiled with anger and sulked outside the house. The more he thought about it the more outrageous it seemed. He had done what was right and proper, but it was his careless, free-spending brother who got his father's love and attention. Jealousy and rage burned in the older brother's heart.

This parable had a special meaning for the early Christians. They were surprised to see how many Gentiles became fine Christians. Greeks and Romans who had led wasteful, immoral lives came to faith in Jesus Christ. They received the gifts of the Holy Spirit. But Jews, who had known the promises of God in the Law and the Prophets, turned their backs on the GOOD NEWS of the kingdom. They thought that they deserved God's love because they kept the Law faithfully and stayed in the household of God. Yet they closed their hearts to the great love of God who is as ready to forgive us as was the father in the parable. He is ready to accept us before we ask for forgiveness.

In the Parable of the Prodigal Son Jesus drew a picture of the forgiving love of God. It is a story that anyone who has ever wronged his parents or who has ever been a parent of a wayward child can understand.

31. Two Who Prayed*

The Temple was a great shrine for sacrifice and prayer. It was not like a church with services and preaching. Rather, everything centered around the bloodstained altar and the fragrant smoke of the altar of incense. At any time of the day, people could enter the great courtyard of the Temple and offer their prayers. They liked to do so because in this holy place the worshipers felt closer to God.

It is our custom to kneel and pray silently. But in Jesus' day, it was the custom to stand and spread out one's arms in prayer. A person spoke his prayer out loud; anyone who was nearby could hear it. Pious Jews developed the art of composing and offering beautiful prayers, like the psalms in the Old Testament. Most of the psalms are prayers of pious and good people. The Jews assumed that God was particularly pleased by the prayers of God-fearing sons of Abraham.

Jesus told a story that surprised and shocked his listeners. In this story he pictured the familiar sight of a fine, respected Pharisee who went to the Temple to offer his prayers. Jesus saw such people before him. They were faithful, God-fearing men—but they were also proud and self-righteous. They said that God has no love for a sinner. They often recited the words of Psalm 5:

> *Thou art not a God who delights in wickedness; . . .*
> *thou hatest all evildoers.*

* The Parable of the Pharisee and the Publican is in Luke 18:9-14. Compare it with Luke 7:36-50.

Or from Psalm 24:

> *Who shall stand in his holy place?*
> *He who has clean hands and a pure heart. . . .*

All who heard the story Jesus told could measure themselves by it. They could decide whether they were as proud and self-righteous as the Pharisee who prayed so eloquently and devoutly: "God, I thank you for helping me to be such a good man. I am not like other people. They cheat and steal; they are careless about the Sabbath; they have affairs with women. But I am different. I fast two days every week although your law does not require so much fasting. I give a tenth of all my income although your law says I need only give a tenth of my crops." On and on he went as he recited his virtues.

Or the listeners could decide whether they were as "poor in spirit" and as "meek" and humble as the tax collector who could only pray, "God, forgive my sins."

Jesus brought the GOOD NEWS of the kingdom in a way that forced everyone to examine himself. The GOOD NEWS is that God forgives (justifies or accepts) only the person who is repentant and humble. God forgives the one who trusts entirely upon His mercy and not at all upon his own goodness.

When Jesus finished the parable, he moved on to other matters. He left the parable to stick in his hearers' consciences. He allowed each person to decide for himself what he must do.

32. The Secrets of the Kingdom of Heaven*

There is a solid, down-to-earth feeling about the stories Jesus told. He had a strong imagination as any good storyteller must have, but he kept his stories within the bounds of ordinary life.

---

* Explanations of why Jesus spoke in parables are given in Matthew 13:10-17; Mark 4:10-12; and Luke 8:9-10.

He did not use anything that was fantastic or unnatural. He told no fables of animals talking or tales of weird, impossible things happening as myths and fairy tales often do.

It would be possible for a painter to take the details of Jesus' stories and paint a panorama of life in Palestine, somewhere near the Sea of Galilee. Such a painting might show a woman tucking a piece of leaven in a batch of dough made from fifty pounds of flour. In a few hours the whole mass of dough would heave and puff up because of the hidden working of the bacteria in the leaven. The painting might include farmers and merchants, shepherds and tax collectors, children playing in the marketplace, and a ragged beggar crouching at the door of a rich man's house. In this painting we would see grapevines and olive trees, mustard plants and the gay flowers of the field, silver coins treasured by a woman and the silver coins handed out by an estate owner to his hired hands at day's end. It would include wedding feasts and banquets as well as common everyday bread and water.

Jesus used familiar things in his stories. His stories were clear, interesting, and easy to remember. Knowing this, no doubt the early Christians asked a difficult question: "If Jesus came preaching the GOOD NEWS of the kingdom of God in stories and parables, why did not everyone understand him?"

The Gospels are the testimony of the early church. They do give an answer to this question, but it is a strange answer. They testify that the kingdom of God did appear in Jesus Christ, but in a hidden way. The secrets of the kingdom were given in parables. Not everyone who heard them could understand or receive what Jesus said. Looking straight at his disciples, Jesus declared:

To you it has been given to know the secrets of
   the kingdom of heaven,
but to them it has not been given. . . .
This is why I speak to them in parables,
   because seeing they do not see,
   and hearing they do not hear, nor do they understand.

The secrets of the kingdom of God were what the disciples discovered for themselves as they pondered the parables of Jesus. When they realized what these secrets were, they also realized that it was God who helped them to understand. More important, the disciples learned the secrets of the kingdom as they sought to obey their Lord, Jesus Christ. The secrets of the kingdom were not bits of book learning. They were learned in the hard business of Christian living and in the personal meetings between the disciples and the great person of Jesus.

What were these secrets?

The disciples learned at least three secrets. First, they learned that God is at work in the world in an unexpected, unpredictable, and surprising way. His kingdom comes and grows as quietly as the seed a farmer sows in his field. The farmer forgets all about the seed, yet night and day it grows. Or the kingdom is like a shepherd hunting in the dark for his hundredth sheep until he finds it, even though the lost sheep could not know where the shepherd was. God acts surprisingly; he looks with favor on the prayers of a sinful tax collector and is unimpressed by the noble prayer of a Pharisee. God is like the employer who paid the same full day's wages to the men who worked one hour as to those who worked the whole day.

Secondly, the disciples learned that God takes all kinds of people into his kingdom. They are invited as the rich man invited people to his banquet. All kinds of people may come into the kingdom, like the fishes pulled into a net, or the field where wheat and tares grow side by side. When the GOOD NEWS of the kingdom comes, it is up to a person who hears it to receive it or to reject it. And the time to decide is *now*.

We can never separate the parables from the person who spoke them. We can separate a great story from the person of the author, but we cannot do the same with Jesus. Behind each parable stands Jesus, our Redeemer. Only with the help of the Holy Spirit can we be moved to faith and understanding.

Thirdly, the disciples learned that in the kingdom things are different. The last will be first, and the first will be last. Sinners will be welcomed because they are humble and penitent, but the proud and self-sufficient will be excluded.

There are many treasures hidden in the parables. Jesus asked his followers to seek and find them there.

VI

GROWING OPPOSITION

33. A Dreadful Certainty

JESUS WAS ONLY TWELVE YEARS OLD when he had to make a hard decision. He had stayed in the Temple while his parents started off on the journey home to Nazareth. The boy Jesus felt that the Temple was the place he should be. It was fascinating to talk to the wise teachers of the Scriptures. His heart was in the study of the things of God. Then his parents burst in upon him. They demanded that he come back with them to Nazareth. They were worried, irritated, and unable to understand the boy. And Jesus obeyed them.

This moment became a turning point in the life of Jesus. Jesus gave up all thoughts of attending the Temple school and went back to life as a carpenter in a country village.

Eighteen years later, Jesus made another great decision. He stepped down into the brown water of the Jordan River to be baptized. He had left behind him the long years of a quiet, ordinary life. At the moment of his baptism, his ministry began. And not long after, Satan attacked him with the temptations in the wilderness.

After each of these two moments, there was no turning back. Each time Jesus made a decision that would influence all that happened afterward.

In the gospel story of Jesus we come to a third turning point. It comes in the middle of the story. This turning point did not come suddenly. Jesus had been expecting it for a long time. When he spoke the Beatitudes in the Sermon on the Mount, he declared, "Blessed are you when men revile you and persecute you. . . ." He had taught his disciples to beware "when all men speak well of you." Jesus had been preparing his disciples for harsh and painful times. Should he not also expect such times for himself?

True, Jesus had friends. A little band of twelve men were loyal to him. But Jesus also had dangerous and powerful enemies. Delegations had come from the high council of Jerusalem to spy on him. He knew that these enemies were filled with fury and were plotting how to destroy him.

When the mob in Nazareth rushed Jesus to the cliff's edge, danger hung in the air. One did not have to be a prophet to see that Jesus was headed for trouble.

The question was, would Jesus try to turn aside? Would he look for a way to avoid a deadly clash? Or would he perhaps find some way to defeat his enemies?

Questions like these must have kept the disciples awake at night. And in hours of quiet prayer, Jesus must have pondered them also. The time would come when he would have to decide. A dreadful certainty arose within him. It was a certainty which would make a strong man tremble. It was the certainty that he would be rejected and ultimately destroyed, unless . . .

How Jesus met this dreadful certainty and how he tried to prepare his disciples for it is the theme of a part of the gospel story which stands like a watershed in the center of Matthew, Mark, and Luke. Beyond that point, the story of Jesus speeds downhill with increasing momentum—to the cross.

34. A Friend Who Doubted*

The old king, Herod the Great, had been dead for many years. He was dead but not forgotten. Before he died the king had ordered that an artificial mountain be built near Bethlehem. That was done and Herod's coffin was buried at its summit. This "mountain" still dominates the landscape south of Jerusalem.

Three of the sons of Herod each got a piece of their father's kingdom. One son was Herod Antipas. He was not really a king, but a "tetrarch" over two territories of his father's kingdom— green and prosperous Galilee to the north and a jumble of rocks and bluffs called Perea, east of the Jordan. Herod Antipas inherited the most powerful fortress of the land. It was Machaerus, perched high on a rocky bluff above the Dead Sea. There Herod Antipas brooded over the vanished glory of his father and held wild parties with his courtiers. The young king shocked the Jews when he brought his brother's wife to the palace to live with him.

While many gossiped quietly in the bazaars, it was John the Baptist who spoke out boldly against the king's sin. John made no effort to be tactful or polite, or even to get out of the clutches of the king. Soldiers came and dragged him away to the fortress. Herod Antipas gave orders to keep him caged up. Herod was afraid to destroy John because everyone revered him as a prophet. He was also afraid to release him.

One day two desert travelers stopped at the guard post below the fortress. "We want to see John the Baptist," they said. Silently and grudgingly the guard waved them on. The words "John the

* The story of John the Baptist's question is told in Matthew 11:2-15 and Luke 7:18-30.

Baptist" opened door after door until the two travelers were inside the fortress courtyard. There they were allowed to peer into the prison cell and to shake the gaunt hand of a man who had despised the houses of men and who had lived bold and free in the desert.

The haggard prophet was worried. Not about himself. Not about the designs of Herod Antipas. He was worried about Jesus, the man he had baptized. Nothing was going as he, John, had expected. Jesus did not preach a thunderous message of doom and judgment. He brought no fire from heaven.

"Tell me," said John in a hoarse whisper, "what is Jesus of Nazareth doing?"

The two men told him about a wedding feast where Jesus had been a guest and wine had flowed like water. John shuddered. He had been content with the sparse food of the wilderness—locusts and wild honey.

"Are there signs of a great baptism by fire?" asked the prisoner.

The two men told him how Jesus held little children in his arms and blessed them. Besides, Jesus did not baptize anybody. John the Baptist was baffled. Nothing he heard about his friend Jesus seemed to make sense.

"Go and ask him outright," ordered the prisoner.

"What shall we say?" the two men asked uncertainly.

"Find him and whisper these words in his ear, 'Are you HE WHO IS TO COME?'" John commanded. This was the question they were to carry back to Jesus.

The two wrapped their cloaks around them and clambered down the steep slopes from the fortress. The dark shadows of the rocks grew and swallowed up the two men. Above in the fortress the prison cell was silent as an unanswered prayer.

Jesus was sad when he heard the desperate question of John the Baptist. It was bad enough when enemies came from Jerusalem and tried to trap him with tricky questions. Now even his friend John was wavering. He had once been bold and sure in the

desert. Now he was filled with doubts. "Are you 'he who is to come'?"

Jesus did not answer this question directly.

Jesus did not proclaim himself a Son of God. As the early Christians remembered it, he simply did what needed to be done at the moment. He comforted the poor. He healed the blind and cleansed the lepers. He let men draw what conclusions they wished. He did not try to glorify himself. Instead, he called himself a "servant" or simply, and somewhat mysteriously, a "Son of man."

Sorrowfully, Jesus told the two men, "Tell him what you hear and see." John must answer his own question.

Then Jesus added, "Blessed is he who takes no offense at me!"

It would always be that way. It would always be easier to forsake Jesus than to believe in him. It would always be easier to doubt than to have faith. But it must have been a heartache to see the iron-voiced desert prophet turn away from Jesus in whom he had placed such high hopes.

By this time a crowd had gathered to hear the latest news about John the Baptist. Then when the two men were gone, Jesus turned to the people and began to preach with the fiery eloquence of the old Hebrew prophets:

"What did you go out into the wilderness to behold?"

Jesus went on to describe John the Baptist. He was not like a reed that bends one way when the wind blows from Rome, another way when it blows from Jerusalem. He was not a man who tried to be popular and please the crowd. At the climax of his speech, Jesus wrapped up in one sentence the greatness and the shortcoming of John the Baptist:

> *Truly, I say unto you, among those born of women*
>   *there has risen no one greater; . . .*
> *yet he who is least in the kingdom of heaven*
>   *is greater than he.*

35. The Fate of a Prophet*

Long ago, after the Babylonians had taken the people of Judea into captivity, the prophet Jeremiah was dragged off to Egypt by Jews who fled from Jerusalem. There, according to Jewish legend, the prophet was killed by his captors. Another ancient legend tells how the old prophet Isaiah was martyred by being cut in half with a saw, like a butchered ox.

In Jesus' day it was taken for granted that a prophet was headed for pain and tragedy. The way the people of Jesus' time read history, it was always true that a prophet was rejected, that people refused to listen, that the doom the prophet foretold was not averted. It was also always true that the prophet refused to give in and that in the long run God's will triumphed. Kings could destroy the prophets, but they could not destroy the Word of God.

Up in the fortress that clung to the cliffs like an eagle's nest, John the Baptist watched each day go by, one like the other. It is probable that he was treated with respect. Even Herod Antipas liked to hear John talk. But there was no sign that either the little king or the great prophet was backing down.

Then one day the executioner came into John's prison cell. In a few minutes the deed was done. As John knelt before him, the executioner swung his sword. Thus the life of the prophet was sacrificed at the drunken whim of a foolish king. All this in a hidden corner of the king's palace.

How this happened is a tale as dramatic as it is outrageous. Herodias was the runaway wife of Philip, Herod's brother; she had become the beautiful mistress of Herod Antipas. She did not like what John the Baptist had said about her scandalous love affair with her brother-in-law. And at a palace party, her chance for revenge came.

* The story of John the Baptist's death is told in Matthew 14:1-12 and Mark 6:14-29.

Wine had been flowing freely at Herod's birthday party. The king may have been drunk as he watched the dance of Salome and swayed to and fro with the music. Salome was the daughter of Herodias (as is known from historical records outside the Bible). Wild with the excitement of the moment and flushed with wine, the king roared his approval.

"Anything you want," he shouted with a string of oaths. "Anything—but don't ask for more than half my kingdom!"

Salome's heart beat fast. She hurried to her mother. "What shall I ask for?" she cried.

This was Herodias' chance and she pressed her advantage ruthlessly. "The head of John the Baptist on a platter," was her grisly demand.

The king had expected nothing like this, but he was afraid to lose face before his guests. The order was given and no time was lost in laying at the feet of the pale dancer the blood-smeared head of the wilderness prophet. The flute players took up gay tunes again, but there was no longer any joy in Herod's palace, or in all his tiny realm.

A day later John's disciples climbed up to the fortress for the last time. Tenderly they carried away the body of the last Hebrew prophet.

36. How They Tried to Discredit Jesus*

The enemies of Jesus were forced to use some indirect methods to combat him. They could not win out when they confronted Jesus face to face because he always took control of the situation. There was something commanding about his person. He knew how to unmask his opponents quickly.

---

* Mark 2:23-28 is one account of the Pharisees' attempt to charge Jesus with breaking the Sabbath.

So it was no accident that Jesus' enemies chose to attack him as a Sabbath-breaker. They knew that if this charge could be made to hold, they could have Jesus expelled from the synagogue. That would mean that he would be cut off from "the people," that is, the people of God. He would not be allowed to enter the synagogue. He could not explain the Scriptures there. He would be branded as a sinner and a lawless man.

One day as Jesus and his disciples walked across a wheat field, the disciples picked a few stalks of wheat. They rubbed the grains loose in their hands and ate the kernels. There was only one thing wrong with this. It was a Sabbath. And picking grain was work.

Jesus' enemies were watching. They chose this incident to charge Jesus with a crime against God.

Jesus had a bold answer. He did not deny the charge. He did not claim that the disciples' actions violated no law. Instead he made the astounding claim: "The sabbath was made for man, not man for the sabbath; so the Son of man is lord even of the sabbath."

Jesus spoke with such power that the plan to discredit him shriveled up and came to nothing.

37. What Stunned the Temple Police*

There was a Jewish feast which combined the joy which we have at Thanksgiving and Christmas. Children and adults looked forward to this great feast. It was the Feast of Tabernacles. This feast was celebrated in September or October at the time of the grape and olive harvest, and it lasted a full week.

Children loved this feast because the families moved outdoors to live in booths made of branches and leaves. Every day for a

* Read John 7—8 for many details of the conflict between Jesus and his enemies, such as the way Jesus answered the question "How will you make us free? We have never been slaves."

AND AS THEY MADE THEIR WAY HIS DISCIPLES BEGAN TO
PLUCK EARS OF GRAIN. AND THE PHARISEES SAID TO HIM,
    "LOOK, WHY ARE THEY DOING WHAT IS NOT LAWFUL
    ON THE SABBATH?"
AND HE SAID TO THEM,
       "HAVE YOU NEVER READ WHAT DAVID DID,
           WHEN HE WAS IN NEED AND WAS HUNGRY,
       HE AND THOSE WHO WERE WITH HIM:
           HOW HE ENTERED THE HOUSE OF GOD,
      WHEN ABIATHAR WAS HIGH PRIEST,
          AND ATE THE BREAD OF THE PRESENCE,

WHICH IT IS NOT LAWFUL FOR ANY
BUT THE PRIESTS TO EAT,
AND ALSO GAVE IT TO THOSE WHO WERE WITH HIM?"

AND HE SAID TO THEM,
"THE SABBATH WAS MADE FOR MAN,
NOT MAN FOR THE SABBATH;
SO THE SON OF MAN IS LORD
EVEN OF THE SABBATH."

week there were platters of juicy roast meat from the many sacrifices. Everyone could eat and drink his fill.

Adults looked forward to the climax of this feast the way we do to lighting the Christmas tree and opening our presents. The climax of the Feast of Tabernacles came when the priests in Jerusalem carried huge jars of water up from the Pool of Siloam to the Temple. They mixed the water with wine and then, while the crowd waited breathlessly, the priests poured the water and wine in a mighty torrent over the altar. Filled with joy, the priests and the people sang:

> *With joy you will draw water*
> *from the wells of salvation. . . .*
> *"Give thanks to the* LORD,
> *call upon his name. . . .*
> *"Sing praises to the* LORD, *for he has done gloriously;*
> *let this be known in all the earth.*
> *Shout, and sing for joy, O inhabitant of Zion,*
> *for great in your midst is the Holy One of Israel"*
> (Isaiah 12:3-6).

Water and wine, a full harvest—did this not merit praise! There would be enough for the winter; God had blessed his land with life-giving water for field and house. It was said, "No one can know true joy who has not seen the joy of the House of the Outpouring," meaning the flowing waters at the feast.

In the Gospel of John, this rite of the outpouring of wine and water at the great feast (along with the kindling of the four great lampstands in the Temple) is contrasted with the person of Jesus Christ. This Gospel often uses such contrasts to testify to Jesus. At the beginning of his Gospel the evangelist had contrasted Nicodemus (representing the wisdom of the Jews) to Jesus (bringing the wisdom of God's Spirit). In this scene from the Feast of Tabernacles the Gospel bears testimony that Jesus brings more joy than the joy of harvest and a greater outpouring of life-giving water than the outpouring at the Feast of Tabernacles.

The story in John's Gospel unfolds in a way that lets us see the opposition to Jesus swell and grow and reach out to capture and destroy him.

"Go to Jerusalem! Show yourself there! No man works in secret if he wants to be known openly! Show yourself to the world!"

Jesus' brothers taunted him to get out of the villages of Galilee and appear in Jerusalem. This would be the right time. The city would be packed with pilgrims. The high and holy priests of the Temple could see and hear him. In one hour at the feast in Jerusalem more people could see Jesus than in weeks of going around in villages of farmers.

"Go up to the Feast of Tabernacles!" they said impatiently.

But the brothers did not believe in Jesus. And Jesus refused to be driven to make a sensational display of himself. He was not one who did a thing like this because someone else urged him to do it. He simply would not go to Jerusalem to perform miracles.

"Go to the feast yourselves; I am not going up to the feast, for my time has not yet fully come," Jesus said.

But a few days later, Jesus did go. He slipped quietly into the narrow streets of Jerusalem. He took his place with the teachers in the Temple and taught.

No friendly crowds surrounded him. Instead people looked into his blazing eyes and said, "You have a demon!"

Others sneered, "How is it that this man has learning when he has never studied?"

A few protested, "He is a good man." But they were drowned out by many who asserted, "No, he is leading the people astray."

The police who guarded the Temple had their orders. They kept close watch to see that no Gentile crossed beyond a certain line around the Holy House. If any Gentile did, he was to be killed immediately. Every Temple guard was on duty when the big crowds assembled. The guards could not help hearing about Jesus who was teaching in the shadows of the great portico where the teachers usually assembled. But for a time they did nothing.

Some of the people were puzzled because not even one guard appeared to silence Jesus or to lead him off to prison. "Can it be that the authorities really know that this is the Messiah?" people murmured.

Such a thing was impossible, they thought. They knew very well where Jesus came from. They expected that the Messiah would come from an unknown place.

The conflict swirled around Jesus, but he did not retreat. And on the great day of the outpouring, Jesus shouted with a mighty voice that echoed among the pillars:

If any one thirst,
  let him come to me and drink.
He who believes in me,
  as the scripture has said,
"Out of his heart
  shall flow rivers of living water."

This had gone far enough, some of the people thought. "Let that man be arrested," they demanded. But no one dared touch him.

The priests stayed hidden in their luxurious rooms and summoned the guards. "Why did you not bring him?" they hissed.

The guards felt foolish. Their captains finally blurted out an unwilling but telling testimony to Christ: "No man ever spoke like this man!"

38. Cities That Had Their Last Chance*

The Gospel of John testifies that Jesus is the water of life, the light of the world. Yet sadness and bitterness appear in this testimony, for when Jesus appeared in this world, most people turned away in doubt. Others turned against him with hatred and with stones hurled in anger.

Opposition like this was a familiar experience to the first Christians. They proclaimed the GOOD NEWS, but few would listen. Faith in Christ did not come easily.

The bitter truth was that Jesus presented a danger to any town or city he came near. This is what the early Christians testified in the story of the cities that had their last chance. Wherever Jesus went, people had to decide for or against him. Unknowingly they faced a kind of judgment.

A great sadness came into the heart of Jesus when he thought of Jerusalem and of other cities and towns in his beloved homeland. It was as if the people of these cities were driving in the nails of the cross even before the hour of crucifixion came.

Capernaum was one of the most important cities in Jesus' early ministry. Jesus went there frequently when he first began preaching and healing. Apparently he stayed in the house of Peter. Capernaum was called "his town" in the Gospels. People in Capernaum saw and heard Jesus often, but few took the decisive step of faith.

Looking back on those days in Galilee, now gone forever, Jesus uttered a series of woes. A woe is exactly the opposite of a beatitude. A beatitude points to happiness, a woe points to sorrow and condemnation.

"Woe to you, Chorazin!"

"Woe to you, Bethsaida!"

---

* The woes spoken against three unrepentant cities can be found in Luke 10:13-15 and Matthew 11:20-24.

"And you, Capernaum, . . . you shall be brought down to Hades."

This was not a cry of hot anger. Jesus did not rebuke these cities of Galilee because he disliked them, but because he loved them so much. He had spent much of his ministry in these cities, but they had turned their backs upon him. These were cities that had had their last chance and the thought made Jesus sad at heart.

When the early church began, Christians saw how the favored cities of Galilee and other parts of Palestine closed their synagogues to the gospel. Instead it was in pagan cities—Corinth, Antioch, Philippi, Ephesus, Rome—that men and women came to faith. The early Christians often thought about the message of Jesus. Even Sodom and Gomorrah—cities remembered for their wickedness—would have repented had they seen and heard what Jesus had done and said in Capernaum or Bethsaida.

As the opposition to Jesus grew in force, the dreadful certainty of his final rejection became more evident. Time was running out. Soon Jesus would leave Galilee where he had grown up as a boy and where he had begun his ministry. He would never return in his earthly form to these cities.

39. What It Means to Have Faith*

"If the Son of man comes, will he find faith on earth?" Jesus once asked.

It seemed that the Messiah might come and no one would believe in him. Jesus himself was disappointed with the lack of faith, even among the disciples. "Have you no faith?" he asked them in the storm on the Sea of Galilee.

---

* The confession of Peter is a halfway mark in three Gospels: Matthew 16:13-20; Mark 8:27-30; and Luke 9:18-22. See also John 6:66-70 for a similar story.

The Gospel testimony bluntly tells us that faith in Christ does not come quickly. Nor does it come to many. The natural question that arises is: Just how may a person come to believe? How did the disciples—those closest to Jesus like Peter, James, and John—come to faith in Jesus?

Just what does it mean to believe?

Many of the testimonies of the Gospels ponder this question. This problem comes to a focus in the story of Peter's confession near Caesarea Philippi. The story seems to say, "This is what it means to believe. This is what faith in Jesus really is. This is how the disciples came to believe."

Caesarea Philippi was a place which devout Jews avoided if at all possible. It was notorious as the land of a bestial, half-animal god, Pan—a creature with the head of a goat, a nature god who was celebrated in wild revels. It was also here that Herod the Great had built a magnificent white marble temple for the worship of Caesar Augustus.

Caesarea Philippi was a beautiful land of cool green mountains, a garden of Eden with bubbling springs and cold, clear streams. The main highway to Damascus swung through this area after leaving the Sea of Galilee to the south.

Why did Jesus come to visit this foreign land? One reason may have been the danger in the south. Herod Antipas, ruler of Galilee, the same man who had put John the Baptist to death, was dangerously curious about Jesus. The king was worried. He feared that Jesus was a resurrected John the Baptist. To set his mind at rest, Herod was eager to see Jesus. This curiosity was a threat to Jesus' safety. At any time Herod might order his soldiers to arrest Jesus. But in the north, outside the borders of Herod's kingdom, Jesus would be safe.

Or Jesus may simply have paid no attention to the news that Herod wanted to see him. He may have been simply looking for a quiet place to think and pray and plan, a place to prepare the disciples for terrible days to come.

As Luke tells us, Jesus often needed to be alone. He had to think things through. There is a clue as to what was on Jesus' mind now in his earnest, searching question to the disciples: "Who do people say that I am?" It was important for Jesus to know what his people, the Jews, thought of him. He needed to know what results his ministry had produced. And the disciples, who mingled with the crowds, would have heard what people were saying when Jesus was not present. They would have heard things that people would not dare say to Jesus.

In his lonely retreats Jesus had come to a clear answer to the question of his identity. He was sure that he was the Chosen One of God. But Jesus had also come to the strange conclusion that as the Chosen One he would not triumph but would have to suffer and even be killed.

No such thoughts seemed to have occurred to the people. True, they were astounded by Jesus. They knew he was no ordinary person. But they thought that if God were with him, glorious things lay ahead for him.

"He is another John the Baptist," they said.

"He is Elijah, the prophet who was taken up into the sky on a chariot of fire. He has come back again," others maintained.

"He is the great prophet, just as Moses foretold when he said, 'The Lord your God will raise up for you a prophet like me from among you . . .' " (Deuteronomy 18:15).

These were the rumors that the disciples reported. The expectations of the people were high, but there was no hint that they saw in Jesus anything more than a prophet. Amid all this limited belief, would Jesus find any real faith at all?

Jesus turned from the comfortable talk about what other people said to an uncomfortable question: "But who do you say that I am?"

Up to now the Twelve had had plenty to say. Now they fell silent. Each man turned his thoughts upon himself. Each had to decide for himself. No one ventured to speak. The disciples scuffed their feet in the earth and began to look to Peter. He was never slow with his tongue.

Deep from within Peter came the words: "You are the Christ!"

Now the matter was out in the open. A word no one had dared to use before had been spoken. In that moment Peter and all the disciples for whom he spoke, stepped across a dividing line. It was the dividing line between the uncertain crowd and the company of those who have taken the magnificent risk of faith.

There had been so much heartache and sorrow in Jesus' ministry. Now his eyes lit up with joy, like the joy of a shepherd who has found his lost sheep.

> *Blessed are you, Simon Bar-Jona!*
> *For flesh and blood has not revealed this to you,*
> *but my Father who is in heaven.*
> *And I tell you, you are* PETER, (rock)
> *And on this* ROCK *I will build my church,*
> *And the powers of death shall not prevail against it.*

The "rock" was the man Peter, the first to confess faith in Jesus. In that moment the community of those who believe, the church, was born. Peter—the "rock"—had not changed his exuberant, enthusiastic, fast-talking personality. But he was also an apostle; he had stated his faith boldly. On such a person who boldly stated his faith with no if's, and's, or but's the community of Christ was established. This faith was nothing that Peter had achieved by himself. Rather, it was a gift of God.

But what sort of Christ was Jesus? The word "Christ" means Messiah. The Jews had many highly colored ideas of what the Messiah would be like. To most people the Messiah was God's Hero who would win freedom from the Romans and power for the Jews. He would gather the scattered people of God and rule them from the mountain of Jerusalem. The Messiah belonged with triumph, freedom, glory. In the wilderness Jesus had fought against the temptation to become just such a Messiah. Instead, Jesus saw in his dark future a strange and different kind of Messiah—a "Suffering Servant" who would be despised and rejected by men.

Peter's confession was a beginning, the most important beginning since the disciples had left their fishing nets and counting tables to follow Jesus. Jesus insisted that the disciples keep this new faith a secret. They were not to talk to anyone about it. For a time it was to be hidden.

Now Jesus began to teach the disciples secretly. As the Gospels of Mark, Matthew, and Luke testify, Jesus began to reveal deeply troubling thoughts which he had never before expressed except in hidden allusions. He told the disciples that the "Messiah" would not be victorious, that he would be defeated and destroyed.

To Peter this just did not make sense.

Was it not true that the Messiah was the Chosen One of God?

Was it not also true that God is all-powerful? Psalm after psalm, Scripture passage after Scripture passage spoke of the triumphs of God and his gracious promises for the future. When the Messiah comes, God will not be defeated.

Therefore, victory must follow the coming of the Messiah just as surely as day follows the rising of the sun.

Peter leaped to his feet and grabbed Jesus by the arm. "God forbid, Lord! You shall not be rejected and killed!"

Peter was sure he was right. He trusted in God. He believed in Jesus. And yet so soon he was betraying his faith in Jesus, the Christ.

"Get thee behind me, Satan!" Jesus said with intense emotion. "You are a hindrance to me; for you are not on the side of God, but of men."

The words were like a slap in the face.

Peter was stunned.

It was a long time before Peter learned the full meaning of faith in Jesus. Not yet had he learned that faith is truly a gift of God, that faith must always obey the unsearchable and surprising will of God.

40. Mystery of the Transfiguration*

Even today, anyone who travels north from Palestine to Damascus is sure to come under the spell of *the* mountain. Arabs call it *Jebel Sheik* (Mountain of the Old Man). All the way to Damascus it is visible on the horizon. Sometimes sudden clouds hide its summit, but often, even in the hot, parched summer, a boy herding goats on the plain or a girl carrying water can see the dazzling snow on the summit. The people in the fields on the plain may never climb that great mountain in the blue distance, but they never forget that the mountain is there. And some may dream of climbing to its top some day.

In Bible times this great mountain was called Mount Hermon. The disciples who had gone with Jesus into the region of Caesarea Philippi could not have failed to look often at the snowy peak which commanded the landscape. When Peter looked up into the eyes of his Master and made his great confession, he may have seen that mountain brooding over the wide landscape in the far distance.

On this mountain, or on another nearby, three select disciples had a strange and mysterious experience.

Jesus selected Peter, James, and John—only these three—to accompany him. The four men went up to the lonely heights to pray. As they climbed in silence, they left behind the ordinary things of the day—cooking breakfast over an open fire, buying bread in a village, bathing in icy, spring-fed streams. For hours no word was spoken. Peter and the others struggled to keep up with Jesus, not only in climbing but also in the wordless hours of prayer. It was very difficult. The disciples grew short of breath as they climbed; they were exhausted by their efforts to pray. Drowsiness overcame them and they longed to lie down and sleep.

---

* The story of the Transfiguration is told in Matthew 17:1-13; Mark 9:2-13; and Luke 9:28-36.

Then a wondrous thing happened. It was as if the three disciples stepped out into a golden sea of light. The past centuries of Hebrew history seemed to collect like rays of light into two balls of fire on either side of Jesus. The figure of Jesus itself changed into a dazzling whiteness, brighter than sun on snow and ice. Two shining, unearthly beings took form at his sides in the blinding light, displaying themselves as Moses, the great giver of the Law, and Elijah, the great prophet.

Words fail to describe the power and feeling of the vision that came to the disciples between waking and sleeping. A cloud of mystery surrounds the story in the three Gospels. We cannot expect the words of the Gospels to describe in photographic detail what the three select disciples glimpsed in a glowing moment as they stood between heaven and earth on that high mountain.

Peter muttered, like a man in a sleepy daze, that this was a good place to be. They must quickly set up three huts to shelter the glowing, ethereal three. Peter did not really know what he was saying. Like the other disciples, he was thoroughly frightened.

As the vision brightened with a fire not seen on earth, something happened that terrorized the disciples as it would have terrorized any man, for the Jews feared God so much that they never dared speak his name aloud. A cloud of light swirled around all three and out of it came a divine voice, the same voice that Jesus had heard at his baptism:

This is my beloved Son;
listen to him!

With the voice the vision vanished as suddenly as it had come. The mysterious experience may have lasted only a second, like the appearance of the risen Jesus to the disciples at Emmaus. It was as if the three disciples had looked beyond their moment in time into the future glory of the risen Lord.

The evangelists expected the readers of the Gospels to understand, knowing that the cross was not the end and knowing the GOOD NEWS of the Resurrection. But at that moment on the mountain, the disciples were unable to understand. They mumbled like men in their sleep. They were still far from understanding what Jesus was saying about his death and suffering, just as they could not grasp what it was that Elijah and Moses said to Jesus in the vision.

What did these two representatives of the old covenant speak about with Jesus? There is every reason to believe that they spoke about the coming death of the Messiah signifying that all Scripture—"Law" and "Prophets"—pointed to the cross. In all its mystery, the Transfiguration gave divine approval to Jesus' alarming and disturbing purpose to go to Jerusalem and confront his enemies in the climax of his ministry.

41. The Bitter Cup*

The disciples of Jesus were flushed with embarrassment. Confidently they had tried to heal an epileptic boy. They had laid their hands on his head. They had done all that they had seen Jesus do, but nothing had happened. The boy did not get better at all. People in the crowd began to titter and laugh at them.

Just at that moment Jesus arrived with Peter, James, and John. He had come down from the mountain and found the excited crowd gathered around the sick boy. Jesus took command of the situation. To the father who cried out to him in faith and also in unbelief, Jesus was loving and understanding—he healed the boy. But for the others he had a stern word. He called them "faithless." He even scolded the disciples for their "little faith."

Nevertheless, in the days that followed a fire of excitement burned in the hearts of the Twelve. They were dazzled about the future, even though they could not understand all that Jesus said

* The story of the bitter cup is told in Matthew 20:17-28 and Mark 10:32-45.

about what would happen. They had heard him promise to give them "the keys of the kingdom of heaven." Before them danced glorious hopes of power and honor at the right and left of the Messiah in his glory.

Who would have the top rank? Would it be Peter? Or would it be the brothers, James and John?

Probably each could think of many reasons why he should be favored—and why the others should have lesser honors.

When Jesus was absent, the disciples began to argue. The dispute reached such a stage that James and John got their mother to ask Jesus for a special favor. She asked Jesus to give the highest honors to her sons.

All those days and weeks Jesus had been thinking disturbing thoughts of the true fate of the Messiah in this world. How often he had tried to explain to the disciples how it would be in the kingdom of God! Once he tried to make it plainer than plain. He picked up an urchin playing in the dust and held the startled child in his arms.

"Unless you turn and become like children, you will never enter the kingdom," he said.

This time Jesus faced the ring of bold and ambitious young men standing around him. He was thinking of what would happen in Jerusalem and asked, "Are you able?"

"Able to do what?" asked the disciples, drawing together shoulder to shoulder.

"Able to drink the cup that I am to drink?" said Jesus. He was thinking of the cup Isaiah had described, a cup of suffering. Isaiah had called it the terrible cup of "staggering," the cup of the wrath of God (Isaiah 51:17).

The eyes of the disciples shone with loyalty and love for Jesus.

"We are able," they chorused as one man.

The time would come when they would have to drink that cup of suffering. It would come in the hard years of the beginning of the Christian church. It was not in Jesus' power to promise honor

and privilege. Jesus must have wondered if the disciples would
ever learn that:

> *Whoever would be great among you*
>   *must be your servant,*
> *and whoever would be first among you*
>   *must be slave of all.*
> *for the Son of man came not to be served*
>   *but to serve,*
> *and to give his life*
>   *as a ransom for many.*

VII

JOURNEY

TO JERUSALEM

42. Galilee to Bethany*

LUKE, THE EVANGELIST, started a complicated task. He promised
Theophilus "to write an orderly account . . . of all that Jesus
began to do and teach" (Luke 1:3; Acts 1:1). The problem was
to decide in what order to arrange the many stories and sayings
of Jesus which Luke had collected. Which came first? Which
belonged toward the end?

Another evangelist had already written the Gospel of Mark.
His work was a help to Luke. Using the Gospel of Mark as a
guide, Luke could arrange the stories and sayings of his collection
in an orderly sequence. This worked quite well up to the time of
Peter's confession at Caesarea Philippi. All the accounts of the
last week in Jerusalem, the Crucifixion, and the Resurrection
obviously belonged at the end of Luke's first volume. But Luke
still had a great deal of material left over. It was enough to fill
one-third of a scroll.

The Gospel writer held in his hand a number of the sayings of Jesus, written neatly on papyrus. In one he read about the three men who came to Jesus and asked to become disciples. "Foxes have holes, and birds of the air have nests; but the Son of man has nowhere to lay his head," Jesus answered.

As Luke studied this material, he found clues for arranging it. It seemed to fit into a long and somewhat zigzag journey from Galilee southward to Bethany, which was two miles east of Jerusalem. This part of Luke is often called the "Perean Journey" because some of the events are said to have happened in Perea—the country east of the Jordan. (Other events in these chapters are not located in any definite place.) In this part of Luke's Gospel we have a general picture of an eventful journey of Jesus across the Plain of Esdraelon between Galilee and Samaria, then across the Jordan to Perea and ending finally in the events at Jericho. At that point Luke's story parallels those of Matthew and Mark and begins to tell the last events in Jerusalem.

A grim foreboding appears in this journey as Jesus moves southward and comes nearer and nearer to Jerusalem. Luke hints at this foreboding in the words *when the days drew near for him to be received up*. Christians in the early church clearly understood these words. As they read each story, they knew that step by step Jesus was coming nearer to the cross where he would be "received up," as well as nearer to the mountain of the ascension where he would be taken up into heavenly glory.

As the early Christians read the stories of Luke, they heard not only the earthly Jesus speaking to the people of his day, but also the risen Lord speaking to them as well. Because of his cross and resurrection, every word of Jesus had a special meaning. To read *he set his face to go to Jerusalem* means more than that Jesus

---

* The story of Luke's "Perean Journey" begins with Luke 9:51 and continues to Luke 18:14. It takes up approximately ten chapters of the Gospel.

traveled southward. To a Christian it also means that Jesus was on a last journey—a journey to his death.

The story of that journey comes to a close with some surprising events in Jericho and in Bethany.

43. Blind Bartimaeus and Rich Zacchaeus*

Of all the persons in the great crowd of people with Jesus in Jericho, none seemed more unlikely to receive special attention than two men. One was a blind man who crouched under a coarse and ragged mantle at the roadside. The other was one of the richest men in Jericho, short and energetic Zacchaeus. Each was an outcast in a special way, and to each Jesus gave something that changed his life forever.

Jesus caused a sensation in the vicinity of Jericho. A crowd of Passover pilgrims gathered to walk with him. The disciples formed a bodyguard. The excitement of getting so near to Jerusalem for the Passover was contagious. As they walked, the people no doubt had important things to discuss with the famous teacher from Nazareth.

Along the way a hoarse cry disturbed the crowd. It came from a heap of rags at the roadside.

> *Jesus,*
> *Son of David,*
> *Have mercy on me!*

The people with Jesus turned toward that heap as a man turns to a barking dog. "Be silent!" they ordered. But the rasping shouts only grew louder.

"Call him," said Jesus.

The heap of rags straightened up to show a man underneath.

* The story of Bartimaeus is told in most detail in Mark 10:46-52. See also Luke 18:35-43. The story of Zacchaeus is told in Luke 19:1-10.

He tossed off his mantle, jumped up, and groped his way toward the kindly voice.

The beggar had just one chance and he made the most of it. "Master," he pleaded, "let me receive my sight."

As Jesus had done many times before when he saw such complete faith, he said, "Go your way; your faith has made you well."

In Mark's Gospel this is the last event before the great week in Jerusalem. This fact is a signal to the reader to stop and look more carefully at the story. We may imagine the early Christians doing so. As they did they would notice that many of the people around Jesus were blind to him. In contrast, a beggar with sightless eyes was able to see with the inner eye of faith. Jesus once said,

> *For judgment I came into this world,*
> *that those who do not see may see,*
> *and that those who see may become blind* (John 9:39).

Those early believers would also notice that the beggar greeted his Lord with the title of the Messiah: "Son of David!" This foreshadowed the glory of Jesus as it would appear in the happenings in Jerusalem. More than that, Bartimaeus did not go back to his old ways, but "followed him on the way."

To this often-told story of blind Bartimaeus, Luke added a new story. It is the story of short Zacchaeus of Jericho.

Jericho was a garden city in the deep, humid Jordan valley, where it was warm even in the wintertime. Soldiers, merchants, and travelers of all kinds funneled through this city on their way to and from Jerusalem. No matter which way the traffic moved, the Roman tax collectors made a profit.

Zacchaeus was not an ordinary tax collector; he was "superintendent of taxes." He had paid a big price for the right to collect taxes in the whole region. As superintendent he was allowed to subcontract tax collecting to minor officials. The disciple Matthew had been one such official, although he did not work under Zacchaeus. Zacchaeus was a short man, but in the tax business he was a "big wheel." He made a handsome profit with little work. The more taxes the Romans demanded, the richer Zacchaeus became. Tax collectors in those days made sure they took in more taxes than they had to hand over to the Romans. What was left over was their profit.

Zacchaeus had a fine name; it meant "pure" or "just." But when he walked through the crowd, people often sneered. "Little Zacchaeus! The pure—pure as the mud in the Jordan!" Months before, some of the tax collectors had gone down to hear John the Baptist preach and had asked him what they should do. John told them to take no more money than was just—exactly the opposite of what most of them were doing. But to be fair to Zacchaeus, we must admit that the Gospel does not make him out to be a scoundrel.

Zacchaeus only wanted to see Jesus. He had no idea of talking to him but simply perched in a tree where he could comfortably overlook the crowd and watch all that Jesus did. Jesus might have walked on by, but the man in the tree caught his eye.

To the surprise of the crowd, Jesus did something that not only startled Zacchaeus but was also sure to make enemies. Jesus invited himself to be a guest in Zacchaeus' house.

This was against every rule. Jesus waited for no invitation. And he chose the worst man to associate with in Jericho. Zacchaeus slid down the tree with joy and put his house at the disposal of Jesus. While the disciples relaxed under the palms of a fine garden and servants hurried to bring in trays of delicious food, the crowd peered through the gates and muttered in disgust, "Guest of a sinner!"

Inside, the short man stood before Jesus in a way that made the little man seem taller and taller. "Here and now, I am going to give half of my possessions to the poor. Those whom I have cheated I am going to repay four times over!" (Old Testament law required a thief to repay four times the amount which he had stolen.)

Zacchaeus well knew that he had done nothing to deserve Jesus' favor. He had not invited Jesus. He had made no amends for his sins. It was Jesus who invited himself into Zacchaeus' life and took him just as he was—Jericho's most hated sinner—even before Zacchaeus made any promises.

This was a happy day for Zacchaeus. Jesus, too, rejoiced. "Today salvation has come to this house," he said with a smile in his eyes for the little man, "since he also is a son of Abraham."

"A son of Abraham! This rich thief? Humbug!" muttered those out in the streets. They could not understand a Savior who came "to seek and to save the lost"—even a man who did nothing to deserve salvation!

What happened to Zacchaeus after this? If Luke knew, he took no space in his Gospel to tell Theophilus about the man. Perhaps he did not need to, because all he wanted to do was show his friend the Man who came, not to those who were satisfied in their goodness, but to those who could only reach out with empty hands to receive what Jesus came to give.

44. Incredible Miracle at Bethany*

The story of Jesus in the Gospel of John moves up to the last week in Jerusalem in a very different way from the other three Gospels. The other three Gospels tell a series of events, one after the other, but the Gospel of John stops to look very carefully at one incredible miracle. This miracle took place in Bethany, a village on a shoulder of the Mount of Olives, just a short walk

---

* John 11 tells in detail the story of the raising of Lazarus. Every part of this chapter has a special meaning which can be discovered only after careful study.

from Jerusalem. Through this miracle shines the mystery and glory of One who is the "Life" of the world. The Gospel of John is built around seven great signs or miracles. The sign at Bethany is the last and the greatest.

"Lazarus is sick," said the women at the well in Bethany. Every day they exchanged news of the village. They pitied his two sisters, Mary and Martha.

"They have sent a messenger to Jesus of Nazareth," someone said.

"Little good that will do," was the reply. "If that teacher comes here, the authorities in Jerusalem will kill him."

A few days later a mournful cry echoed up and down the streets of the little village. "Lazarus is dead."

In a few hours the last rites for the dead were over. In Bible times, the funeral began immediately after a person's death.

Mourners gathered at the house and began to yell and scream as was customary. The louder the yells and screams, the greater the honor to the dead person. Grief-stricken friends of Lazarus also came from Jerusalem to do him honor. The body was washed and anointed. Then it was wound tightly from head to toe with linen strips. All the villagers followed the procession that carried the cloth-wrapped corpse to the burial cave. When the body had been placed inside, they watched the men roll a heavy stone to seal the opening and keep out any animals of prey.

Still there was no word from Jesus.

Jesus had heard the news of his friend's illness with a strange calm. "This illness will not end in death," he said. His disciples thought he meant only that Lazarus would soon get well.

They could not understand what Jesus meant. "It has a purpose. It will be the means by which God will make himself known through his Son." This they could not understand because they did not yet have the key to understanding. Readers of John's Gospel have the key; it is the cross and the Resurrection. The resurrection of Jesus unlocks the meaning of the incredible events in Bethany.

Finally Jesus announced that it was time to go to Bethany. The disciples were alarmed. It would be dangerous to go so close to Jerusalem.

"Are there not twelve hours of daylight?" Jesus said. As long as the appointed "day" of his life lasted, Jesus would be safe. When that day came to a close, then the powers of darkness would take hold—but not until the appointed hour.

Jesus' words were like riddles to the disciples. But they did understand when he said bluntly, "Lazarus is dead." They had no idea what Jesus meant when he said he would go to wake him out of his sleep. Thomas, the pessimist, knowing that the disciples could not hold Jesus back, said to the others, "Let us go and die with him."

Jesus arrived in Bethany at the most dangerous and yet the most favorable time. It was favorable because whatever Jesus did or said would be seen and heard by large numbers of people. A great crowd of friends had come from Jerusalem to comfort the two sisters in their sorrow. It was also dangerous because the authorities in Jerusalem could not ignore Jesus' presence. If he were nearby, they would have to act against him.

Martha ran to be the first to greet Jesus. Full of sorrow, she reproached him, "Lord, if you had been here, my brother would not have died."

Martha did not stop with this reproach. "I know that whatever you ask from God, God will give you."

Like the disciples, Martha was not able to understand Jesus, not even when he said, "Your brother will rise again." No one— not energetic Martha, not quiet, thoughtful Mary, not the closest friends of Jesus—was prepared to see the incredible power of God in Jesus.

Martha's ears rang as she heard Jesus declare, "I am the resurrection and the life. . . ." Jesus said that a person can have the life that he gives even though he sleeps the sleep of death.

"Do you believe this, Martha?" Jesus asked.

THEY TOOK AWAY THE STONE.

AND JESUS LIFTED UP HIS EYES AND SAID,

    "FATHER, I THANK THEE THAT THOU HAST HEARD ME.

    I KNEW THAT THOU HEAREST ME ALWAYS,

    BUT I HAVE SAID THIS ON ACCOUNT OF THE PEOPLE

      STANDING BY,

    THAT THEY MAY BELIEVE THAT THOU DIDST SEND ME."

WHEN HE HAD SAID THIS, HE CRIED OUT WITH A LOUD VOICE,
　　"LAZARUS,
　　COME OUT."
THE DEAD MAN CAME OUT, HIS HANDS AND FEET BOUND
WITH BANDAGES, AND HIS FACE WRAPPED WITH A CLOTH.
JESUS SAID TO THEM,
　　"UNBIND HIM, AND LET HIM GO."

"Yes," she answered, "I believe that you are the Messiah, the Son of God." She spoke the words, but she could believe only in part, and her despair was not driven away.

Jesus did not go into the village. He waited at the edge of Bethany while Martha quietly summoned her sister Mary. Mary ran with Martha, and the curious crowd tagged along behind them. Jesus saw the commotion and the tear-streaked faces of the sisters. In the two sisters, the neighbors, and the crowd Jesus saw a wall of doubt, grief, and spiritual blindness surrounding him.

Jesus groaned with a kind of inner anger. His body shook with a powerful emotion. He was "deeply . . . troubled." He, too, began to weep, and the tears he wept seemed to the onlookers like tears of sorrow, but they were really tears of bitter anger and exasperation.

Jesus ordered the men to open the burial cave, unmindful of the crowd's protestations that the body was decaying. Then Jesus raised his face to the sky in prayer.

With a mighty shout, Jesus summoned Lazarus from the tomb: "Lazarus, come out!"

One would think that the stiff figure that appeared at the tomb opening would have made all the crowd believe in the power of God in Jesus. Yet the Gospel of John declares that the miracle only made the enemies of Jesus more determined to destroy him! The miracle of Jesus was too great to be understood, both for his friends in Bethany and for his enemies in Jerusalem.

Jesus had once promised his friends that when he was gone, the Holy Spirit would come to guide them in all truth—but that time had not yet come. Until it came, the miracle remained incredible.

VIII

PARTING FROM THE

DISCIPLES

45. Only in Jerusalem

"IT CANNOT BE THAT A PROPHET should perish away from Jerusalem."

That was what Jesus once said when well-meaning Pharisees whispered a warning in his ear. They had come to tell him that Herod Antipas was looking for him.

As the opposition to Jesus grew stronger, Jesus knew that the day must come when he would have to stand up to it. He could not stay in the villages of Galilee; he would have to face his nation and his enemies in the city of Jerusalem. No doubt Jesus thought of Jeremiah, who long ago had uttered dangerous words near the king's palace in ancient Jerusalem. Only in Jerusalem could Jesus speak to the whole nation, for that city was the center of the life of every devout Jew.

The time had come. Now Jesus was approaching the Holy City. There he would proclaim his message of the kingdom of God—

the GOOD NEWS. There he would have to face the men who hated him most—the Pharisees and the Sadducees, the scribes and the Herodians, the priests and the great high priest himself.

Long ago, according to the story in the Book of Jonah, the people of Ninevah had repented when the prophet Jonah had preached to them. Jesus hoped with all his heart that his nation would listen to him. He was not simply going through the motions of proclaiming the GOOD NEWS; he yearned for his people with his whole being. He had come not to condemn but to save, not to judge but to bring salvation.

The story of what happened when Jesus did appear in Jerusalem and faced his nation and his enemies is arranged in a neat pattern in the Gospels. It begins with our Palm Sunday and moves through the days of the week to Maundy Thursday—the evening of the Lord's Supper. This pattern makes it easy for Christians to remember those events, although they may actually have happened over a longer period of time. The week began with joy and

song as Jesus entered Jesusalem, but it turned to bitter tragedy on Thursday night when Jesus ate his last meal with his disciples and the hour of parting from them approached.

46. Why Jesus Chose a Donkey*

Donkeys were as common on the roads of Palestine as cars are on our streets today. These uncomplaining, cheap little animals were good for one thing: bearing burdens. They could also be used to ride on, but riding a donkey is not easy for an adult. You have to straddle the little beast and hold your feet out wide so that they do not scuff on the ground, and turn up your toes so

* Luke 19:29-44 tells how Jesus answered the Pharisees who wanted him to quiet the crowd. This passage also describes other ways in which Jesus spoke and acted like a prophet.

that your sandals do not jiggle off. It is almost impossible to sit on a donkey and look dignified. The fuzzy, friendly animal seems so small that you might think a grown man who rides him ought rather to be carrying the donkey!

Jesus decided to ride a donkey into Jerusalem. It was not because he was tired and the road was uphill. It was not because he was in the habit of using a donkey for his travels. Rather it was because Jesus planned his entry into Jerusalem carefully. This was a time when everything he did and said was watched by a thousand critical eyes. What Jesus did was well thought out and deliberate.

No one could mistake the meaning of the donkey, trotting along with the broad-shouldered carpenter on its back, or straining to climb the slopes to the city walls. No one, that is, of the many pilgrims who were coming to Jerusalem for the Passover Festival. All along the way these devout people had been singing psalms and reciting the ancient promises of God. They remembered what the prophets had said, and as they thought of the Old Testament prophets, they saw Jesus acting like a prophet himself.

Sometimes the prophets of old acted out their messages. For example, Jeremiah once slung a wooden ox yoke around his neck and walked through Jerusalem. He did so to tell the people that they would soon be under the yoke of Babylonia. Isaiah made an unforgettable impression when he walked through the streets of Jerusalem barefoot and almost naked, like a prisoner of war. This was the way he told the people that the Assyrians would take them captive.

Jesus had no such grim message to tell by riding a donkey.

Instead, he acted out a message of joy. He was acting out the prophecy of Zechariah: "Tell the daughter of Zion, 'Here is your king, who comes to you in gentleness, riding on an ass, riding on the foal of a beast of burden' " (*New English Bible*). Jesus was acting out the prophecy of a Messiah who would come in meekness, not in pride, riding on a war horse. This Messiah King would bring peace and rule with justice, so the prophets had foretold.

The people with Jesus rejoiced. They caught the spirit of what Jesus was doing and turned the procession into a parade. Off came their coats—red, blue, and brown. With shouts of joy they carpeted the ground with their coats. For flags and banners, they pulled down leafy branches from trees and bushes and waved them in the air. They sang and shouted:

Blessings on him who comes as king
in the name of the Lord!
Peace in heaven,
glory in highest heaven! (*New English Bible*)

Songs from the psalms accompanied the man on the donkey.

All this could not pass unnoticed. Jesus spoke and acted like a prophet. He caught the attention of Jerusalem. Some Pharisees rushed to the gate and told Jesus, "Make those people keep quiet! Stop this nonsense!"

But who could ever tell this man what to do, or spoil the joy of the festive entry into the city on Mount Zion?

47. What a Prophet Would Do in the Temple*

There was only one place in Jerusalem that really interested Jesus—the Temple. The first thing he did after he made his festive entry into the city was to go to the Temple and look around. Then he left the city to spend the night in Bethany, probably at the house of Mary and Martha.

The next morning Jesus returned. He loved the Temple. Many years before when he had visited the Temple as a twelve-year-old,

* The most detailed story of the cleansing of the Temple is in John 2:13-22. See also Mark 11:11, 15-19.

he had called it "my Father's house." But what Jesus saw this time filled him with anger. Instead of a place of quiet for prayer he walked into a building as noisy as the midway of a county fair. Once inside the gate he was surrounded by the bustle of a livestock market.

The gate of the Temple opened into a large enclosed square, several acres in extent. This part of the Temple was open to the general public. It was called the Court of the Gentiles. On all sides around the outer edges were "porches" supported by tall stone pillars. People came and went at any time of the day. Within this paved area stood the complex of buildings that surrounded the Temple itself. One inner court was for women, the other for men. There were also storage rooms for the use of the priests. Rising above these stood the golden-roofed Temple and its mysterious "Holy of Holies."

Jesus stopped in anger and amazement. Around him was a jumble of livestock dealers, pens of bleating sheep, cages of fluttering pigeons, and all the smells and dust and noise that went with the business of selling animals for sacrifices. Prices were high here, but that was part of the business which the priests controlled. For a higher price than outside the Temple a pilgrim could buy an animal already inspected by the priests and approved for sacrifice.

Who could pray here with the shouts of money changers in his ears, yelling to attract customers? Excited pilgrims crowded around to buy the proper Jewish coins—the only kind accepted for paying the Temple tax or for offerings. Roman and Greek money was branded as idolatrous and unclean because the coins bore the "graven image" of a king. Graven images were strictly forbidden by the Ten Commandments. The pilgrims were too excited to know whether they got a fair exchange, which added still more profit to this Temple trade. Yes, who could pray here where men were haggling, bargaining, and swindling each other?

What Jesus did at that moment was as startling as the eruption of a volcano. He stepped forward like a mighty Elijah and shouted, "Is it not written, 'My house shall be called a house of prayer for all the nations'? But you have made it a den of robbers." Picking up rope used to tie sheep for sacrifice, Jesus made a whip which he swung around his head. With a clatter he upset the tables of the money changers and herded the merchants before him like a flock of frightened chickens. From one end of the great court to another he marched, and no one dared stop him. No one dared resist because the power and authority of Jesus overawed them.

The way Jesus cleared the Temple was a dramatic way of saying that God was now sending his Messiah. Jesus acted as if the Temple were *his house*. God meant it to be used for worship, for getting ready for the coming of the Messiah. Jesus acted the way a prophet would act, with vigor and boldness. People remembered the words of Malachi:

> . . . *The Lord whom you seek will suddenly come to his*
> *temple. . . .*
> *But who can endure the day of his coming,*
> *and who can stand when he appears?*
> *For he is like a refiner's fire . . .* (3:1-2).

48. The Herodians Spring a Trap*

The money changers picked up every rolling coin and the pigeon dealers recaptured their fluttering wares. Jesus had cleared the Temple courtyard, but the merchants soon set up business outside the Temple—and the next day they were probably back in the Temple court again. As long as sacrifices went on, as long as hundreds of thousands of Jewish pilgrims came to Jerusalem, such a business was necessary.

* The story of the question about tribute money is in Matthew 22:15-21 and Luke 20:20-26.

Jesus had acted forcefully and dramatically in clearing the Temple courtyard of merchants and money changers. He was not afraid of the gathering storm and came to the Temple each day.

The question now was what the men higher up would do. The Temple authorities could not let this challenge pass. They soon appeared and began to heckle Jesus on one key point. They demanded to know by what authority he, a country carpenter, presumed to teach and give orders in matters of religion. Behind this attack was the unspoken question *Who is this man?*

Jesus stood boldly and publicly in the Temple, just as any other teacher of the things of God. What he had to say he said in the open where all could hear. His enemies came to him in the Temple. There followed many a duel of question and answer. Sometimes this fencing ended abruptly when the questioners were confounded by a question which Jesus asked them and which they were afraid to answer. But there were always others ready to step up and try to confuse or discredit or ridicule Jesus.

Now a group of smiling, polite men approached Jesus. They were known as "the Herodians." They belonged to a political party which supported the kings which the Romans had set up, such as Herod Antipas. Their motto was "Don't upset the apple cart." They were all for "things as they are now"; they wanted no change. They wanted to keep peace with the Romans.

The Herodians were smooth talkers. They were pleasant and friendly in manner and approached Jesus with compliments and flowery words. They addressed him respectfully as "rabbi." They acknowledged him to be a blunt and honest man. "You care for no man," they said, praising Jesus. "You teach the way of God truthfully."

To all this Jesus could not say "no." He was indeed truthful. He was not awed by a man's position or wealth. He did teach the way of God. The disciples, also, had to agree, but they were uneasy. The Herodians were too oily in their manner.

The Herodians wanted to flatter Jesus. Flattery, they thought, would lead him into their trap. Once they could spring their trap, Jesus could not get out, either by saying "yes" or by saying "no."

To understand the clever trap that the Herodians thought up, it is important to remember that the Jews in Palestine had to pay several kinds of taxes to the Roman government: a ground tax amounting to one-tenth of the taxpayer's grain and one-fifth of his oil and wine; an income tax amounting to about 1 per cent; a poll tax amounting to one denarius per person. (A denarius was the average pay for a day's work.) Each person had to pay this tax every year.

No matter what kind of tax it was, the Jews hated to pay taxes to their Gentile overlords. But it was also most dangerous to oppose the Romans. Roman power was built on the flow of taxes from the empire. On the other hand, each time a Jew paid his taxes, he felt as if he were paying tribute to a hated foreign ruler.

After the Herodians had warmed up with their flattering talk, they were ready to spring their trap. "Is it right to pay the tax, or not?" they asked. (By "the tax" they probably meant the poll tax.) They thought they had Jesus cornered. If he said "no," they could accuse him before the Romans of being a subversive. If he said "yes," they could accuse him of being a traitor to the Jewish people.

Jesus was not at all flustered. He called for a denarius and let the men look at the image of Caesar's head stamped on the coin. Those who could read deciphered the Greek inscription *Tiberiou Kaesaros*—"of or belonging to Tiberius Caesar." Jesus let the coin give an answer.

"Pay Caesar what is due to Caesar," he said. Caesar had ordered these coins to be minted; he maintained the government; he provided peace and safety for his realm; he had the right to receive taxes from the people in return.

"Pay God what is due to God." It was as if Jesus were saying, "You also have a duty to God."

49. A Joke for the Sadducees*

In matters of religion and politics, the Jewish people of Jesus' day did not see eye to eye. Normally, the Herodians, the Pharisees, and the Sadducees were constantly quarreling. Now, however, they all went after Jesus like a swarm of hornets. The Pharisees, especially, hoped to push Jesus into some blasphemous statement about his divine authority—that is, blasphemous to a Jew. In their common enmity for Jesus, the Sadducees put aside their differences with the Pharisees. But they could not help being pleased when they saw how the Pharisees had failed when they went after Jesus with their questions.

The Sadducees decided to play a joke which would make both Jesus and the Pharisees look ridiculous. As they plotted their prank, they must have chuckled and rubbed their hands. Their plan seemed foolproof.

Everyone knew how the Sadducees differed from the Pharisees. The Sadducees had a short "Bible" of only five books (Genesis to Deuteronomy), but the Pharisees accepted a longer "Bible" containing many other sacred books such as the Prophets, the Psalms, and other writings. At the time of Jesus, the full number of books for the Jewish Bible (our Old Testament) had not yet been officially established. The Sadducees and the Pharisees got into quarrels about newer teachings which were based on the larger "Bible" of the Pharisees and upon other traditions. One such newer teaching was the doctrine of life after death and a resurrection from the dead.

When the Pharisees got together, they liked to debate all sorts of questions about the resurrection. They debated whether or not a person would rise from the dead with clothes on, and if he wore clothes, whether they would be the clothes in which he had been

* What happened when the Sadducees tried their joke is told in Matthew 22:23-33.

buried or some other garments. The Pharisees went on to maintain that the resurrection would take place in Palestine only. If a Jew were buried outside Palestine, they believed his body would roll through caves under the ground until it reached the Holy Land for the resurrection.

As far as the resurrection was concerned, Jesus sided with the Pharisees, but he did not give his approval to their weird attempts to explain details.

A Sadducee, hearing the word "resurrection," would snort in disgust, "Nonsense, there is no resurrection!" He would point out that nowhere in Scripture (the Books of the Law) is there a single word to support such a new-fangled idea.

Knowing that Jesus believed in the resurrection, the Sadducees were all set for their joke.

"First we will get him to agree on the law about marrying a widow," said the ringleader of the Sadducees.

"He will have to admit that if a man dies childless, someone has to take care of his widow," said another.

"That's right. The next unmarried brother must marry that widow. The family must not be allowed to die out because there is no child," said a third Sadducee.

"He will agree. Then we will tell our story," said the ringleader.

"What story?" someone asked.

"It goes like this. There were seven brothers. The first took a wife and died without children. Then the second brother took the widow as his wife, but after a while he also died without children. Then it was the third brother's turn. The same thing happened again, and so on until all seven brothers had married the same woman. Finally the woman died."

"Aha!" said several with glee. "Then we will spring the question: 'At the so-called resurrection, when all seven brothers come back to life, whose wife will that woman be?' "

The Sadducees grinned. To their way of thinking, it would be a fine joke if Jesus would have to make the ridiculous assertion that in the resurrection a woman might have seven husbands! The Sadducees had perfected their scheme. Now they waited for a chance to corner Jesus and enjoy their joke.

"Everyone in Jerusalem will be laughing at him," said their ringleader.·"And at the Pharisees, too!"

50. Parables of the Sudden Hour*

Each day during that last week in Jerusalem Jesus and his disciples went into the city and spent the day in the Temple. In the morning as the disciples entered the great bronze gates, they took pleasure in the beauty of the Temple.

"Look, Teacher, what wonderful stones and what wonderful buildings!" said a disciple.

There was good reason for his comment. Herod the Great had started a remodeling project to make the Temple one of the most magnificent structures of the world. He had extended the great court and had made the great sanctuary more massive and splendid than it had ever been before. This building project went on after the old king's death and even at this time it had not yet been completed.

The Temple seemed as solid and permanent as the promises of God. Lovingly, the disciples let their fingers ripple over the giant pillars. The disciples felt as if they were walking in a wide, safe place. God would always guard and keep the Holy House in Jerusalem. To Jesus, however, no human structure was permanent.

"The time will come when not one stone will be left upon another," he said.

* Mark 13 gives a long account of the coming tribulations and the judgment. Matthew 25:31-46 describes the surprising judgment of God on the last day. Matthew 24:45—25:13 records two Parables of the Sudden Hour.

Jesus knew that his nation was like a multitude rushing down a road that ends at the edge of a precipice. If they did not halt, they would plunge to their destruction. Jesus foretold a day of ruin and of great tribulation. That day did come in the year 70 when the Romans crushed a Jewish revolt and leveled the city of Jerusalem. The early Christians remembered this terrible event as they read the Gospels.

Not only did Jesus talk about the coming doom for Jerusalem, but he also spoke about the sudden hour for which his followers must always be prepared. Sometimes he talked about the fearful end of the world and the great judgment of God. Then the Son of man would come in his glory and all the angels with him. As a shepherd separates sheep from goats, the heavenly judge will separate the blessed from the damned. His judgment will be a surprising one.

The disciples asked curiously, "When will the Messiah appear?"

Jesus warned them that this question was unimportant and unanswerable. Much more important was the question "Will you be ready for the sudden hour?" Jesus asked this question in the form of two parables.

One parable was about a clever servant and a foolish servant. While their master was away, the clever servant always kept himself ready for his master's unexpected return. The foolish one was careless, and when the master suddenly arrived he found him drunk and unprepared.

The other parable was about the maidens at a village wedding. They wanted to be in the wedding celebration when the bridegroom came to take the bride to his house. First they had to wait until the festivities in the bride's house were over. That could take a long time. Then there would be shouting and merrymaking as the joyous villagers accompanied the happy pair to the bridegroom's house for the feasting.

The maidens, as Jesus tells the story, were ready, each with her clay lamp. Each poured olive oil into her lamp and then lit the wick. Some thought, "It won't be long." They were the foolish maidens. Some were not so sure, so they took extra oil.

At midnight the news traveled up and down the village street: "The bridegroom is coming!" By this time the oil in the lamps of the foolish maidens was used up. Without burning lamps they could not join the parade.

The sudden hour had come. It was too late to fetch new oil. It was not possible to borrow from the others. The five maidens who were prepared followed the bridal couple into the house and the door was shut. The others could not come in.

When Jesus had finished telling the story, he did not have to explain what it meant. The coming of the glorious kingdom of the long-awaited Messiah might be delayed. At the sudden hour when it comes, it will be a calamity for those who are not ready.

"Watch therefore," said Jesus, "for you know neither the day nor the hour."

51. Everything She Had*

Jesus' last days in Jerusalem were brightened for him by several deeds of devotion. Amidst the deadly enmity of the Pharisees, Herodians, and Sadducees, these deeds shone like bright flowers along a desert path. One day little children chanted their "Hosannas" to Jesus. The scribes were annoyed, but Jesus did not let the scribes silence the children. Jesus enjoyed their gaiety. It would be wrong to silence them. Jesus was especially touched by the deeds of devotion of two women. What each of these women did seemed foolishly extravagant, yet Jesus praised their extravagance as the right thing to do.

---

* Deeds of devotion: songs of the children, Matthew 21:14-17; the widow's two coins, Mark 12:41-44 and Luke 21:1-4; the anointing at Bethany, Mark 14:3-9 and Matthew 26:6-13.

"OUR LAMPS ARE GOING OUT;
GIVE US SOME OF YOUR OIL."
"NO," THEY SAID;
"THERE WILL NEVER BE ENOUGH FOR US BOTH.
YOU HAD BETTER GO TO THE SHOP AND BUY
SOME FOR YOURSELVES."
WHILE THEY WERE AWAY THE BRIDEGROOM ARRIVED;
THOSE WHO WERE READY WENT IN WITH HIM TO THE
WEDDING; AND THE DOOR WAS SHUT.

AND THEN THE OTHER FIVE CAME BACK.
    "SIR, SIR," THEY CRIED,
    "OPEN THE DOOR FOR US."
BUT HE ANSWERED,
    "I DECLARE, I DO NOT KNOW YOU."

KEEP AWAKE THEN;
    FOR YOU NEVER KNOW
THE DAY OR THE HOUR.

One day Jesus sat in the inner court of the Temple where he could watch the people come and go. He watched as they put their offerings into the treasury. On top of each treasury chest were gaping bronze funnels, shaped like horns. He could hear the coins rattle down the funnels and drop into the chests below. Rich men came and poured out their gold to the applause and approval of those who watched, but Jesus kept silent.

All kinds of people passed by. As was his custom, Jesus looked for the poor and neglected. In Jericho he had seen Zacchaeus up in the tree. Now in the Temple court he watched a poor widow. She was happy to drop her tiny bit—two copper coins—into the treasury. It was not the amount of the gift, as the money changer would reckon it, that counted before God. Solemnly Jesus said to his disciples:

I tell you, this poor widow has put in more than
   all of them;
   for they all contributed out of their abundance,
but she out of her poverty put in all the living
   that she had.

Probably the widow did not even hear what Jesus said. She did not need to hear, for her reward was that her offering was pleasing to God.

The other extravagant deed took place in Bethany, the village where Jesus was accustomed to stay. During the Passover week there was much feasting in the village. People regarded it an honor to invite a "rabbi"—a teacher of the things of God—to their festive meals. Simon, called "the leper," gave Jesus a seat of honor at a rich meal in his house. Simon seems to have been a wealthy man; he may also have been a Pharisee. We can imagine his guests seated in the courtyard of his house near a cool fountain while they enjoyed the leisurely meal.

People could look in from the street. One person not only looked in, but walked in with a lovely, fragile vase in her hands. It was a creamy white jar of the finest marble, called alabaster because it was quarried in Alabastron in Egypt. A cloud of fragrance accompanied the woman. The jar was filled with a costly ointment, distilled from an herb called nard which grows only in the high Himalayas of India.

Those who were money-minded could quickly calculate the cost of the eggshell-thin jar and its expensive perfumed oil—more than a laborer's wages for a whole year.

"Worth 300 denarii if it's worth a penny," calculated a dark-browed man.

"Enough to put on a feast like this for 5000 poor people!" said a man who was good at doing sums in his head.

Ointments were one of the luxuries and delights of the Mediterranean world. Fragrant and soothing, they took away the harsh sting and burn of the scorching sun and sandy winds. Men and women alike found pleasure in the aromatic oil that trickled through their hair and gave forth a sweet, clean fragrance after a parching day. The carvings on a chair that belonged to King Tutankhamen of Egypt show a young wife anointing the head of her royal husband.

The woman marched straight to Jesus and broke the jar open to anoint his head—not with just a dab, but with the entire contents.

The guests sucked in their breath with amazement.

"What a waste!"

"Foolish extravagance!"

Simon, the host, was embarrassed. He had neglected the courtesy of anointing his guest as a good host should have done.

Jesus silenced the grumbling men. His words were as gracious as the act of the woman:

She has done a beautiful thing to me.
For you always have the poor with you,
  but you will not always have me.
In pouring this ointment on my body
  she has done it to prepare me for burial.

52. Judas, the Betrayer*

The disciples saw the woman empty the alabaster vase of ointment on Jesus' head. According to the story as it is told in the Gospel of John, it was Judas Iscariot who objected to the scandalous waste of this expensive ointment. He saw only the monetary value of the gift, but there was a deeper meaning in the act of anointing. Kings were anointed to reign. Priests were anointed to serve. Altars and holy objects were anointed, also. The very word "Christ" or "Messiah" means "the anointed one." The woman's deed meant, "I know that you are the Messiah and that you are soon to die."

The woman who anointed Jesus may not have known that Jesus would soon die, but the first Christians knew it as they read the story in the Gospels. The anointing was a hidden testimony to the GOOD NEWS in the atoning death of the Christ.

Judas muttered and did not understand. His misunderstanding was deeper than ignorance. John's Gospel says harshly, "He was a thief." Judas became the betrayer.

But why did Judas want to betray Jesus?

Judas remains a great mystery, as unfathomable as the mystery of Satan who tried to tempt Jesus in the wilderness and at many other times.

The Gospels have more to say about *how* the conspiracy to betray Jesus was formed than *why* Judas became the key person in the betrayal. At the time Jesus was feasting in Bethany, Caiaphas, the high priest, called a secret meeting in Jerusalem. The purpose of the meeting was to devise a way to destroy Jesus. The Jewish religious leaders knew what they wanted to do, but they did not know how they could do it safely. They could, at any time, send guards to arrest Jesus and put him in prison. If they did so, they could be sure of one thing—a tremendous riot in the Temple.

---

* The conspiracy to betray Jesus is described in Matthew 26:1-5, 14-16.

There were many there who loved Jesus as deeply as did Bartimaeus who had received his sight, or the woman who had anointed him in Bethany. A riot and tumult could easily backfire upon the priests and exalt the power of Jesus. It was not impossible to imagine the mob driving the priests from their stronghold and making Jesus their hero and leader.

The priests also thought about the Roman soldiers who kept watch from a fortress tower overlooking the Temple. They would surely come swinging their swords and trampling the mob under the hooves of their horses. The Temple itself might be endangered.

Any way they looked at it, it was a risky project. Yet they were determined to destroy Jesus, and they felt they must do so quickly.

Just at that moment Judas shuffled into the inner chamber of the priests. He had a proposition to make.

"What will you give me if I deliver him to you?" he asked.

The Gospels are not quite clear at this point. Matthew puts the money first and the plot second. Other Gospels put the plot first and the reward second. It is hard to imagine why Judas agreed so quickly to betray his Master for thirty pieces of silver. That was the price of a slave, according to Old Testament standards. It was a tenth of what the woman's costly ointment had been worth!

The enemies of Jesus now had an ally hidden among the closest and most trusted friends of Jesus. With Judas' help it would only be a matter of time until they could seize Jesus in secret and act before any of his friends could foil their scheme.

This was a real betrayal. The Gospel of Mark makes that clear. Judas was not pretending to betray Jesus while still secretly loving him, doing what he did only because he wanted to force Jesus to display his divine power and show himself as the Messiah. Matthew hints that Judas did what he did because he wanted the money. The Gospels of Luke and John peer into the mysterious darkness of Judas' plot and say that this was the work of Satan, who had entered his heart. The Gospels do not go beyond a few hints, and these are not enough to explain this mystery of evil.

53. Bread and Wine of the "New Covenant"*

Judas walked along with Jesus and the rest of the disciples as if nothing had happened. At his belt the leather bag with the thirty silver coins grew heavier and heavier. For a moment it seemed like a millstone, but then he shook off the idea and continued to pretend to be a disciple.

In this week before the Passover, Jesus planned carefully how he could be alone with the twelve disciples at an evening meal. It must be inside the city of Jerusalem—not in Bethany. It must be private and undisturbed. Arrangements had to be secret. The way the place for the meal was selected was almost like a conspiracy. Only two disciples knew in advance where it would be.

"Go into the city," Jesus said to Peter and John. "Look around until you see a man carrying a jar of water. Follow him."

Fetching water was a woman's job. A man with a water jar would be as conspicuous as a man in our day carrying a woman's handbag.

Peter and John were instructed to follow the man in silence. They were to follow him into a house, where they were to speak the password: "The Teacher says to you, Where is the guest room? . . ." The owner of the house would show them the place. This hidden room in the upper story of a house in the crowded city became the famous "Upper Room" of the gospel story.

Was this a full Passover feast, complete with roast lamb and all the special dishes of that festive meal? Or was it simply a meal during the Passover week? The Gospel stories differ at this point.

---

* The oldest written account of the Lord's Supper is in 1 Corinthians 11:23-26. The Gospel accounts, which were written later, are in Matthew 26:17-29, Mark 14:12-25, and Luke 22:7-23. John's Gospel has no account of the Lord's Supper, but there are allusions to it in John 6:47-58. The incident of the foot washing is told in John 13:3-15. How Jesus foretold his betrayal by Judas is told in John 13:21-30.

If Peter and John were to prepare for the Passover meal, they had plenty to do. There were many things to get ready for the complicated menu that never changed from year to year. They would have to get a bowl of salt water to place on the table. This was the bowl of tears—the tears of the Israelite bondslaves in Egypt under a long-ago Pharaoh. Four cups of wine were needed to be passed around at the proper times. Water for washing hands according to Jewish ritual had to be provided. Someone had to make a sauce of dates, raisins, and vinegar. Another bowl of bitter herbs was needed—horse-radish, chicory, endive, hore-hound. At the feast each person would dip a bunch of herbs into the sauce—herbs as bitter as the slavery in Egypt and sauce as thick as the clay with which the Hebrew slaves had made bricks in Egypt.

When the second cup of wine was passed around for all to drink, the youngest would ask, "Father, what do you mean by doing this?" And the father—or the host at the meal—would answer as he did each year, "It is the sacrifice of the Lord's Pass-over, for he passed over the houses of the people of Israel in Egypt when he slew the Egyptians but spared our houses." Then the company at the meal would sing a song of praise called a "hallel." In Hebrew "hallel" means praise. The disciples probably sang the words of Psalm 113, which begins "Praise the Lord!"

Then the ritual of the meal would continue until all the roast lamb had been eaten and the four cups for the four promises of God had been drunk. For the Jews, the Passover meal was a meal of rejoicing. For a company of thirteen men, Peter and John would need much help to get everything ready.

On the other hand, if it were only to be a quiet supper in the Passover week, the preparation would not be so difficult. Accord-ing to the Gospel of John, this was a meal *before* the Passover, and the *Crucifixion* also came before the Passover was eaten.

People in Jesus' time ate slowly and in a very relaxed way. As the disciples came to the secret room, they stretched out on couches or pillows around a low, U-shaped table. They took their places just as they came from the street, stopping only to wash their hands—from the fingertips to the wrist, from the wrist to the fingertips—as was the Jewish ritual before meals.

No one volunteered to fulfill the customary duty of bringing a bowl and a towel for washing and drying the feet. Any disciple who did that would be acknowledging that he was less important than the others. All aspired to the top rank in God's kingdom. None wanted to be lowest. In fact, the disciples took up their smoldering argument about who would be the most honored in the kingdom when it came in its glory.

Jesus rose from the meal and, like a servant, washed the feet of the disciples. He went from one to the other like a lowly slave. It was an unforgettable and solemn parable in action. In his deed Jesus repeated what he had often told his disciples: "Whosoever would be great among you must be your servant."

Now that the dust of the street was washed away, the men took their places at the meal again. Judas sat nursing his dark thoughts. He could not help noticing that Jesus was unusually pale and disturbed. The Master had set his heart upon this meal, but he seemed unusually shaken. It was like no other meal, but the disciples could not understand why. Usually, when the wine goblet was passed around, there was laughter and merriment. Instead, while they were eating, a great sorrow came over Jesus.

"One of you will betray me," he said quietly.

This upset the disciples. Question after question tumbled from their lips. But Jesus did not answer directly. "It is one who is dipping bread in the same dish with me," he said.

Could Judas have dared to look into the troubled eyes of Jesus? By what Jesus said he would know that Jesus knew his shameful secret.

As the men ate together, Jesus did two things which they were never to forget. Both were utterly simple and natural things to do. At any meal of this kind, it was the duty of the host to break the

loaves of bread before giving them to his guests. He did so because knives were never used at a meal and bread was not sliced as it is today. It was also the duty of the host to say a blessing over the cup of wine each time he passed it around. Jesus had broken bread many times with his disciples. He had done this in an especially memorable way when he fed the multitude in the wilderness.

This time Jesus broke the bread again as he was accustomed to do. He spoke the usual Hebrew blessing, but he had more to say. "Take, eat," he said simply, "this is my body." As the bread had been broken, so his body would be broken in his death.

Then Jesus took the cup of wine and offered the usual prayer of thanks. As he handed the cup to the disciple next to him to start passing it around, he said, "Drink of it, all of you."

Jesus went on to say in measured words, "This is my blood of the *covenant*. . . ."

Covenant—that was a word often on the lips of the Jewish people. They were proud to be "people of the covenant." The covenant lifted them above all other nations of the world. They were the chosen people because of the covenant. A covenant was a solemn promise and agreement. The greatest example of God's covenant was his solemn promise and agreement through Moses on Mount Sinai—the old covenant or "testament" of the Law.

The Jewish people liked to look back upon this great covenant, but the prophets had also looked forward to a "new covenant." Jeremiah foresaw a new covenant which would replace the old one. There, in the Upper Room behind closed doors, Jesus spoke of the "new covenant" or "new testament" which would be established by his blood and his death.

The gospel story moves on swiftly because there was much more to tell. The time came, however, when Christians turned back to this story of the Last Supper with new understanding. They called it the "breaking of bread" or the "meal of the Lord" or a meal of "communion with Christ." Finally they called it the Sacrament of the Lord's Supper.

All this lay in the future, however. When the meal was finished, the disciples stood up and sang together Psalm 113 once more,

Praise the LORD!
Praise, O servants of the LORD,
praise the name of the LORD!

Then they went with Jesus out into the night.

IX

FROM GETHSEMANE

TO GOLGOTHA

54. The Last Twenty Hours

JESUS AND HIS DISCIPLES sang the joyful "hallel" to its last line. Then they left the Upper Room and stepped out into the dark. If Jesus and his disciples had done what was customary for them, they would have gone to Bethany to spend that Thursday night. Every evening of that week they had left the crowded and noisy city, overflowing with pilgrims, to spend the night in that village.

The disciples were weary. The excitement and strain of the days of danger were telling on them. They felt drained of strength and exhausted by the intense feelings of the evening meal with their Master. For a short time they felt buoyed up by the words of Psalm 118 which they sang for the Passover:

It is better to take refuge in the LORD
    than to put confidence in princes.

But now the disciples wanted just one thing—a quiet place to stretch out and sleep. Instead Jesus looked for a place to pray.

This was the hour of darkness, and the forces of darkness were massing for their greatest attack.

That night there would be no rest or slumber for Jesus. The speed of the events of the final moments of his life would allow him no peace. From the prayer vigil under the shadowy olive trees in Gethsemane to the tree of the cross and then to the tomb in the garden of Joseph of Arimathea, we can number hardly more than twenty hours. These are the great twenty hours toward which the gospel story has been moving from the beginning. They are the hours Christians celebrate on Maundy Thursday and Good Friday.

> *O sinful man,*
> *It was the ban*
> *Of death on thee that brought him*
> *Down to suffer for thy sins*
> *And such woe hath wrought him.*

55. Under the Olive Trees*

In the Upper Room Jesus had given a signal to the man who would betray him. It had been a last warning to Judas just before it was too late for him to turn back. But the warning had been in vain. Judas had left the Upper Room to help Jesus' enemies. He did not stay in the company of the Twelve.

Jesus turned to another of his disciples—Peter—and warned him, also. It was a warning not only for Peter, but for all the disciples.

"You will all fall away because of me this night," Jesus said.

Peter was very sure of himself. "The others may," he said, "but I will never fall away." Peter had been the first to make the great

* The story of the arrest in Gethsemane is told in all four Gospels. Mark 14:32-52 and John 18:1-12 supply many of the details.

confession. He was stoutly confident that Jesus could count on him.

"The rooster will not crow three times this very night before you will deny me three times," Jesus said quietly.

"Even if I must die with you, I will not deny you," Peter said.

Afterward Peter remembered that Jesus had said he was praying for him lest Satan gain full power over him. Jesus knew the weakness of Peter. He knew that bold words do not always result in steadfast deeds. He knew how easy it is for a man to talk big, but in a time of testing, to act small.

On the way up the slope of the Mount of Olives, Jesus turned aside and entered the stone gate of an olive grove. People called this grove "Gethsemane," which means "olive press" in Hebrew. Perhaps it was a garden belonging to a wealthy friend in Jerusalem who allowed Jesus to stop there any time he wished. Jesus liked the place because it was quiet and secluded. Once inside under the trees, the disciples dropped to the ground and made themselves comfortable. But Jesus would not allow three of them to stay there—Peter, James, and John. He took them with him into the shadows of the grove.

"Keep awake with me," Jesus begged his three friends. The three men tried to do so. They could hear Jesus praying a short distance away. He did not stand upright with his face turned to the sky as was the Jewish custom. Jesus was bowed to the ground as if the weight of the whole world pressed upon his shoulders.

A word from his childhood prayers came to Jesus' lips. "Abba!" he cried. He spoke in Aramaic, the language of the Jewish home. He used the word of a trusting child for his beloved father, "Abba!" In all that Jesus said there breathed the spirit of the simple prayer he had taught his disciples, which begins, "Our Father."

The disciples had seen Jesus shaken in spirit when he stood before the grave of Lazarus at Bethany. Now they saw him shaken even more deeply in the hour of his greatest agony.

It seemed to Jesus that a terrible cup was being pressed to his lips. It was the cup of suffering which would soon be his when he fell into the hands of cruel and brutal men. This was a bitterness greater than the bitterness of pain and death. Would that God would cause it to pass from him! He did not want death. He did not want defeat.

And while Jesus wrestled in prayer, the three friends began to snore. Jesus came back to wake them once, and again a second time.

Jesus cried out to God. It was like beating one's fists at heaven's gate for an answer. But no answer came to his prayer. Jesus faced the awesome mystery of God's will. And he bowed to the mystery of God's will with words he had taught his disciples to pray, "Thy will be done." God would not take away the terrible cup of suffering.

A third time Jesus shook Peter and the other two. The men were dazed and unprepared, but Jesus was alert, calm, and ready. "The hour has come," he said simply.

Jesus knew that it was his hour because of the noise. A little army of men had clattered into the grove—a detachment of armed Roman soldiers. Armed Temple police and their officers. Men with lanterns. More men with smoking torches. Servants of the priests with sticks and clubs. Even some of the chief priests. Men enough to down the friends of Jesus if they should choose to fight. At the head of this force was Judas, who stepped up to the erect figure of Jesus and planted a kiss upon his head, as it was the custom to do for an honored rabbi.

It was a kiss of treason and betrayal.

Soldiers rushed to grab the disciples and cut off their escape. Just as quickly Jesus stepped forward and identified himself.

"I am Jesus of Nazareth, if that is whom you want. Let these men go!" Jesus said with poise and calmness. Such a show of force was not necessary. Had he not taught publicly in the Temple every day?

AND IMMEDIATELY, WHILE HE WAS STILL SPEAKING,
JUDAS CAME, ONE OF THE TWELVE,
AND WITH HIM A CROWD WITH SWORDS AND CLUBS,
FROM THE CHIEF PRIESTS AND THE SCRIBES
AND THE ELDERS.

NOW THE BETRAYER HAD GIVEN THEM A SIGN, SAYING,
"THE ONE I SHALL KISS IS THE MAN;
SEIZE HIM
AND LEAD HIM AWAY SAFELY."

Peter rushed in to defend his Master whirling a sword like a windmill. A servant in front of Peter dodged, escaping a crushing head wound. But the point of the sword sliced off his ear.

"No more of this!" Jesus ordered. He healed the frightened servant's wound almost before the man could realize what had happened. In the meantime, the disciples scattered like frightened birds. Before any of the soldiers could seize and fetter them, they were gone in the darkness.

Another young man also ran away, but not quickly enough. A guard grabbed him to pull him back. He wriggled free like an eel and ran away naked, leaving the surprised guard holding his clothes. It may very well be that this man was John Mark. He had probably jumped out of bed in his house in Jerusalem, wrapped a sheet around himself, and hurried out to warn Jesus or to defend him.

From a hiding place in the distance, Peter watched the bobbing lanterns move toward the city. Keeping in the shadows, he followed to see where the Temple police were taking Jesus.

56. Why Caiaphas Hunted for a Crime Against Religion*

Peter crept along on the dark side of the street. He was frightened but persistent. He kept track of the crowd and saw the men take Jesus into the palace of Caiaphas. This handsome and luxurious palace was built around a large courtyard. Peter managed to slip inside. He mingled with the servants and the other people who were coming and going all night.

Everybody in Jerusalem knew Caiaphas, but he was far from a popular man. True, people bowed respectfully whenever Caiaphas walked across the Temple court, wearing the fine robes of

---

* The story of the trial before Caiaphas and Peter's denial is told in Matthew 26:57-75; Mark 14:53-72; and Luke 22:54-65.

the high priest. There had been a time, many years ago, when the high priest was also the king of Judea. Those days had come to an end when the Romans came. The priestly families had stayed on and clung to their dignity, power, and wealth. But the priests were not popular. People hated the family of the high priest. It was said, "Their sons are keepers of the treasury; their sons-in-law are the guardians of the Temple; their servants beat the people with staves."

Priests were rich and powerful, but none was richer or more powerful than old Annas. He had once been the high priest, but when his term ended, he did not give up his authority. He simply saw to it that his son-in-law, Caiaphas, was put on the throne of the high priest. Caiaphas sat on the golden throne, but it was Annas who told him what to do and say.

The two men, Annas and Caiaphas, were determined to destroy Jesus now that they had him in their clutches. Without any delay, Caiaphas called the Sanhedrin for a midnight session. Servants brought lights and chairs into a big room in the palace. Messengers came and went to summon the seventy councilors. Annas and Caiaphas scolded the servants for every delay.

"Pretend to have a trial," Annas instructed his son-in-law. "Never mind that it is not in the Hall of Hewn Stone of the Temple. We will have it right here."

Annas had more to do than summon the men of the council. He called some trusted men of his household. "Bring in some witnesses who will say that we want them to say," he ordered. "Spare no expense to bribe them."

Caiaphas had been high priest for eighteen years. He knew that this could not be a legal trial. Not at night. Not on a festival day. Not without the proper procedures. Not when the judge was also the prosecutor. But there was no time to lose. Caiaphas was uneasy and feared an uprising of the people to rescue Jesus.

Obeying Annas' instructions, Caiaphas looked for a crime that he could charge against Jesus. It must be a crime against religion, for if this could be proved a sentence of death could be justified according to Jewish law.

"Why must this man die?" asked one of the elders.

Caiaphas looked at him sternly. He had explained this before. "It is better to let this one man die than to let a whole people perish!" Caiaphas regarded Jesus as an upstart, an imposter. He feared this man from Galilee because he knew that he endangered the whole priesthood, even the existence of the Temple. Annas and Caiaphas claimed that for the good of the nation, Jesus must die.

What if Jesus were not an imposter? What if he really were sent from God?

Caiaphas dismissed such thoughts. He was fighting for his family, for the priesthood, for the immense wealth that came from the Temple business. All this he could not give up—nor could Annas, nor could the elders and scribes.

Some empty-headed fellows were called to be witnesses against Jesus.

"Let the witnesses come forward," ordered Caiaphas. "What have you to testify against this man?"

First one man was called to testify. "This fellow said, 'I can pull down the temple of God, and rebuild it in three days,'" he said (*New English Bible*).

Then the second was called to testify, but what he said did not agree with the first man's story. According to Jewish law, at least two witnesses were required for evidence in court.

In desperation, Caiaphas began to cross-examine Jesus, even though it was illegal in a Jewish court to force a man to testify against himself. "By the living God I charge you to tell us: Are you the Messiah, the Son of God?" (*New English Bible*).

"You have said so," Jesus answered, and the words of the Book of Daniel came to his lips. He spoke of the Son of man who will come on clouds of heaven.

This set loose a racket of shouts and hisses.

"Blasphemer!" yelled the elders. "The man must die!" The high priest sprang to his feet. Taking hold of his robe at the collar, he ripped it to the hemline. This was his way of pretending to be horrified. The council which had met to hear evidence in a court became a mob. The men spat in Jesus' face. They blindfolded him and roared with laughter as they struck him with their fists and demanded that he "prophesy" who it was that struck him.

Outside the palace Peter strained to hear what was going on. He heard the shouts and feared the worst. No one in the courtyard seemed to have a good word to say for Jesus. They knew how dangerous Annas could be if he were angry.

Peter's thick Galilean accent gave him away. People often said as a joke that Galileans spoke such poor Hebrew that they were unfit to pronounce the benediction in the synagogue. Three times servants and bystanders in the courtyard recognized Peter as a disciple, though he protested with many an oath.

Then it was quiet again in the palace. Far away, chickens stirred on their perches and a rooster gave his thin and penetrating cry. Peter heard, and then he remembered Jesus' words. He could stand it no longer. As he ran out of the courtyard, tears streamed down his cheeks.

57. Pilate's Feud with the Jews

The men who were shouting in the priest's palace and calling Jesus a blasphemer and an imposter, were like dogs that bark loudly but cannot bite. For all their bluster, Annas and Caiaphas had failed. They did not have a case against Jesus which would allow them to rush him out and stone him as a blasphemer. Besides, they could not pass a death sentence. That was something that only the Roman government could do.

Annas was far from giving up. It would be necessary to get Roman support for a death sentence, and he was determined to do just that. At this time of year, the Roman governor was in Jerusalem, although his headquarters were usually in Caesarea on the seacoast. Pontius Pilate, the Roman governor, had come to Jerusalem with additional soldiers to keep order during the Passover Festival. He knew that this angered the Jews because the soldiers could look down on the Temple from their tower fortress.

Years ago the Romans had been satisfied to rule the country through King Herod the Great. This system of ruling through puppet kings had been less successful in the case of Herod's sons. Finally the system had broken down in Judea, and the Romans had sent their own men to rule the country. Pilate was the fifth Roman governor to serve in Judea. He had arrived in the year 26 and managed to keep his job for ten years.

Pilate tried to play the bold, tough governor, but he was not a big enough man to succeed. He hated the Jews, and his fury grew because he was also afraid of them. One time he had sent a company of soldiers into Jerusalem. They had carried their golden eagles and the bust of the emperor inside the walls of the city. This was a deliberate insult to the Jews, who hated any kind of "images." When the Jews protested, Pilate summoned them to meet him in the amphitheater and then had it surrounded by his soldiers.

"Give up your superstitious protests," ordered Pilate, "or my soldiers will kill every one of you."

The Jews laid bare their necks and told Pilate to go ahead. Pilate trembled. To have slain the defenseless crowd would have cost him his position, so he backed down.

The feud between Pilate and the Jews went on year after year. Pilate tried other approaches. He attempted to win the favor of Jerusalem by building an aqueduct to pipe in much needed water. This only earned Pilate more hatred because he used money from the Temple treasury to pay for the aqueduct. Once, in a fit of cruelty, he posted soldiers in civilian clothes among rioting Jews. At a signal, the men fell on the Jews and slaughtered them.

Pilate passed from the pages of history a few years after the Crucifixion. About the year 36 Pilate put down a revolt in Samaria with bloody cruelty. The Samaritans had long been considered friends of the Romans. When Emperor Tiberius heard what Pilate had done, he summoned him to Rome. According to legend, Pilate committed suicide while in prison to avoid execution.

After the hectic night in the palace of Caiaphas, the priests did not have to go far to find Pilate. He was staying in a Roman palace called the *praetorium*. It was in the tower fortress of Antonia, adjoining the Temple. The men from the priest's palace went up to the steps of the *praetorium* and impudently demanded that Pilate come out to talk to them. They did not enter because they dared not "defile" themselves by going into Pilate's house during the Passover. Pilate gave in to their demand and came out, feeling like a man who is bothered by a buzzing fly which he cannot chase away.

58. What Made Pilate Squirm*

Caiaphas did not want a private meeting with Pilate. He took with him all the scribes and elders from the council room where Jesus had been tried for blasphemy. He called his servants from the court of his palace. The Temple police came along and all the motley army of men which had gone out at night to find, surround, and capture Jesus in Gethsemane. Everyone went along.

By the time Pilate came out to the steps, the space in front of the Roman headquarters was jammed with people; Pilate could smell trouble in the air.

There was no bowing and scraping.

There were no polite, smiling words of peace.

---

* Pilate's stratagems for wriggling out of sentencing Jesus to death, are described in Matthew 27:15-26; Luke 23:1-25; and John 18:28—19:16.

The priests and elders elbowed their way as close to Pilate as they could. Everyone tried to speak at once.

"He is perverting our people!"

"He forbids us to pay the Roman poll tax!" At that Pilate lifted his eyebrows in suspicion.

"He says he is Christ, a king."

This made an impression on Pilate. The Romans were always on the alert for any signs of a rebellion. But Pilate was not easily hoodwinked into thinking that the priests were eager to help him destroy a possible rebel.

Pilate looked for the man who was the target of the priests' fury. They pushed Jesus forward. He stood before Pilate with his hands bound like a dangerous criminal. Pilate was an experienced official and he knew how to spot a revolutionary. He looked at Jesus and satisfied himself that the political charges against this man must be trumped up.

The people booed. "He stirs up the people," they shouted. Their mood was ugly and dangerous. Pilate looked for a way out and decided he would simply avoid passing sentence.

"This man is a Galilean. Take him to Herod—it's his business to take care of Galilee."

Herod Antipas was visiting in Jerusalem at the time and Pilate thought he could get rid of the troublesome case by passing it on to him.

Herod was delighted and flattered. He was curious to find out about this man who performed wonders. But the curious king could not penetrate Jesus' great silence. And the Galilean ruler was unwilling to put Jesus on trial. He was disappointed that Jesus would not perform a miracle to please him. His soldiers mocked Jesus brutally and escorted him back to Pilate.

Pilate became more and more uneasy.

The more he saw of the silent, helpless man, Jesus, the more fearful he became. Pilate was sure that the man was innocent of any crime against the Romans. The Gospel stories hint that Pilate

"Ibis ad crucem"

dimly felt that this man was more than a religious fanatic, perhaps more than an ordinary human being. Pilate remembered the troubled dream of his wife, Claudia Procula, and he felt a vague foreboding.

Besides, Pilate hated nothing more than to be pushed around by the Jews.

How this uncomfortable Roman squirmed and twisted to find a way to set Jesus free and to get away from the persistent priests and Pharisees! The Gospel stories tell the story in detail. Each cunning trick Pilate thought up was thwarted by the brutal pressure of Jesus' enemies. Pilate could find no easy way out. If he asserted the minimum truth about Jesus—that he was innocent of any political crime—the Jews could complain to Rome that he had set a "subversive person" free. That would end Pilate's career. On the other hand, if he condemned Jesus, he would be guilty of an injustice.

Pilate tried to sway the mob to pity. He let them look at the whipped, bloodstreaked, and tortured victim. This had no effect. Then he tried to persuade the crowd to accept the release of Jesus instead of a violent and dangerous murderer named Barabbas. Finally Pilate spoke the terrible Latin words:

"Ibis ad crucem" (You will go to the cross).

As Pilate turned away from the nasty scene, he must have felt as if he, not Jesus, had been on trial, and as if he, not Jesus, were the condemned.

59. Ugly Death on a Dump Heap*

Today we speak of the cross as "glorious" and "wondrous." Actually it was, as the Roman statesman Cicero said, "the cruelest, most hideous of punishments." Romans regarded it as "a torture, fit only for slaves." It was a public death reserved only for the worst criminals and for traitors to the Roman power.

Everything about a crucifixion was done to humiliate, degrade, and torture the victim. After sentencing in the courts the victim was turned over to rough and brutal soldiers who were trained to enjoy cruelty. They were allowed to make sport of him in whatever way they wished. Then he was stripped of his clothes, which was the height of shame for the extremely modest Jews who shunned any kind of nakedness. Amidst screams of pain, the victim was spiked alive to the pole and crossbar. A peg, fitted below the groin, helped support the body so that it would not tear loose, yet allow the maximum pain in the festering wounds.

The idea behind this nasty form of execution was to disgrace the victim and his followers and to frighten anyone from the crime of treason against the Roman government. In this case three men were crucified at the same time. Jesus was hung between two notorious criminals. The place of execution was a refuse heap outside of Jerusalem. It was probably a place where the bodies of dead animals were thrown and their whitened bones lay about. Hence, the place was called Golgotha, which means "skull." No pleasant spot was chosen for the Roman crosses.

The soldiers were finished with their beastly task by nine o'clock in the morning. It was only twenty-four hours after Jesus had been teaching the things of the kingdom of God in the Temple.

---

* The four accounts of the Crucifixion are in Mark 15:21-41; Matthew 27:32-56; Luke 23:26-49; and John 19:17-37. Each account is distinctive. Putting all four accounts together gives a composite picture of the Crucifixion.

Usually the victims were allowed to hang on their crosses for days until they finally died and their flesh rotted away in the hot sun. This would not do on the Passover holiday. The priests insisted that the bodies be taken down and the lives of the victims be beaten out with hammers. But by three o'clock in the afternoon this was not necessary to do to Jesus. A soldier pushed a spear into his side and showed that he was dead.

Above the limp body was nailed the sarcastic inscription of Pilate. It read *Iesus Nazarenos Rex Iudaorum*—Jesus of Nazareth, King of the Jews. Pilate put it there to make fun of the Jews, and it had prompted cruel mockery on the part of the bystanders. Christians look upon this inscription as a title of honor and truth. On the cross Jesus became the King of every believer. His shame became the GOOD NEWS of the Christian faith.

60. What Did He Say? *

Each of the four Gospels tells the story of Jesus on the cross in a distinctive way. According to Mark, the oldest Gospel, Jesus hung on the cross as silently as he had stood before Pilate and Herod. He was taunted and mocked, but he made no answer. Then at the last moment, with the fierce strength of a dying man, he shouted the first words of Psalm 22:

> *My God, . . .*
> *my God, . . .*
> *Why . . .*
> *hast thou . . .*
> *forsaken me?*

Psalm 22 was a prayer every Jewish young man learned so that he could use it on his deathbed. With a loud cry Jesus breathed

* The seven last words of Jesus on the cross can be gathered from Matthew 27; Mark 15; Luke 23; and John 19.

his last. The officer in charge was dumbfounded. "Truly this man was a son of God," he said, not caring how strange the words sounded from Roman lips.

The story in Mark is told simply and powerfully. But was this all that Jesus said from the cross?

The other Gospels recall other bits of conversation. Jesus' mind was clear to the end. All together, the four Gospels mention seven times that he spoke from the cross. At one time he turned to answer the plea of the criminal who hung on a cross beside him, "Truly, I say to you, today you will be with me in Paradise." He was saddened by the decision of his enemies and prayed for them, "Father, forgive . . ." He talked to his mother with tenderness, and gave her into the care of the disciple John. He asked for a drink, "I thirst." He recognized the triumphant moment of his ministry on earth: "It is finished." And when he died, he committed himself into his Father's hands.

Christians treasure these "seven words from the cross" as among the most precious sayings of Jesus. Each helps us understand many other things that Jesus said and did. They help Christians think about some of the deeper meanings of the GOOD NEWS of salvation through the cross of Jesus Christ.

X
RESURRECTION
AND ASCENSION

61. From an Earthly Man to a Heavenly Lord

THE GOSPEL STORIES set down clearly and in a matter-of-fact way the harsh, physical details of the Crucifixion. The stories from the four Gospels fit together to describe that event. Then the testimony of the Gospels moves to a new and amazing fact: the Resurrection. Up to this point, the Gospels have presented Jesus of Nazareth, a real person, a man of flesh and blood. Now the Gospels testify to the Christ of faith, a heavenly being who will be with us always, even "to the close of the age."

The Resurrection is like a door that opens into a new world. "We have beheld his glory, glory as of the only Son from the Father," the Gospel of John testifies. In the light of this glory, death is not the end, and the cross is not a tragedy. Rather, the cross becomes a great symbol of the love and purpose of God. All the fears of the disciples, their doubts, their unwillingness to believe were driven away by the new reality of the divine Christ.

In the Gospels we do not have one great story of the Resurrection, but several stories. These stories differ so much that it is better to take each by itself rather than to try to fit them into one connected report. As the Gospel stories move from the tomb of Jesus to his ascension into heaven, they direct our eyes to the certainty of the Resurrection. This is a certainty, but it is also a great mystery. It is a mystery which the Gospels do not explain. They simply state: He is alive! He is with us!

We will move from Mark, the oldest Gospel, to John, the youngest Gospel. Before we do so, we should look at an ancient letter. It was written some twenty-five years after the Resurrection and sums up the evidence for it:

> First and foremost, I handed on to you the facts which had been imparted to me: that Christ died for our sins, in accordance with the scriptures; that he was buried; that he was raised to life on the third day, according to the scriptures; and that he appeared to Cephas, and afterwards to the Twelve. Then he appeared to over five hundred of our brothers at once, most of whom are still alive, though some have died. Then he appeared to James, and afterwards to all the apostles. In the end he appeared even to me . . . (*New English Bible;* 1 Corinthians 15:3-8).

Paul the apostle, who had once been Saul, the Pharisee and persecutor of the followers of Jesus, was the man who wrote this letter in the year 55 to Christians in Corinth.

62. Strange Tale of the Women*

The tumult of Friday in Jerusalem settled into the quiet of the great Sabbath of the Passover. No food was cooked. No work was done. No burdens were carried. No long journeys were undertaken. The silent Saturday passed, and three women waited for

214 / Resurrection and Ascension

sundown when the holy day would come to a close. What they wanted to do could not be done in the dark, so they had to wait until the earliest light of the first day of the week.

They wanted to do Jesus' body the last honors of a proper anointing, not knowing that this had already been done. With Mary Magdalene were two mothers of the disciples—Mary the mother of James the younger and Salome, the mother of James and John.

It would take courage to approach the corpse, to wash it, to spread the fragrant oils and spices, to shroud the cold limbs and look into the face of a dead man whom they had loved.

As the Gospel of Mark tells the story, it explodes as suddenly as a firecracker.

The women dropped their jars and bundles. Their hands shook with fear and their bodies trembled. Frightened out of their wits, they scurried away like rabbits. They were too afraid to tell anyone what they had seen.

Why were they so shocked?

They had seen a man in dazzling white, seated "on the right side" of the tomb. "Do not be amazed; you seek Jesus of Nazareth, who was crucified. He has risen, he is not here. . . . Go, tell his disciples and Peter that he is going before you to Galilee; there you will see him. . . ." *

Matthew's Gospel carries the story a step further. The women actually saw Jesus. He greeted them and they knelt before him and grasped his feet with their hands. And in Galilee Jesus appeared to the eleven disciples on a mountain. Some of the disciples were sure he was there, others doubted it. And with a last word of Jesus, Matthew's Gospel closes. It sums up the duty of his followers as Jesus had been teaching them all his ministry:

> Go . . . make disciples of all nations. . . .
> . . . I am with you always, to the close of the age.

* What the women discovered at the tomb is told in Mark 16:1-8. Other details are added in Matthew 28:1-20.

63. Great News from Emmaus*

"His tomb is empty! We saw it!" said the women. But because they were women, the disciples had their doubts. Like most men of their day, they were inclined to look down upon women. They dismissed the story of an empty tomb as an idle tale. The disciples simply did not believe the women.

This is the way the Gospel of Luke begins its account of the Resurrection. Whether this was an idle tale or not, a rumor or a fact, a vain hope or a certainty, the time had come when it seemed safe for the friends of Jesus to leave Jerusalem. They began to return home to pick up the pieces of a life they thought they had left forever. Two of these friends were going to Emmaus, half a day's walk from Jerusalem. On the way they walked with stooped shoulders and hanging heads. They talked about only one thing— the shocking events in Jerusalem. No matter who joined them and walked along with them, they always came back to the same events. They talked about how they had hoped that Jesus was the one who would redeem Israel. They repeated the strange tale of the women. They reflected upon the words of the prophets about a suffering Messiah. One of the men who joined them had the burning words of Isaiah on the tip of his tongue and recited them. He also repeated many other familiar oracles of Scripture.

As they walked they were so deep in thought that they did not look at each other closely. With customary hospitality the two men invited their companion to stay the night with them. They set a simple meal on the table. Then, without waiting for the host to say the blessing, the guest took the bread, asked a blessing, broke the loaf, and handed the pieces to them. "And their eyes were opened and they recognized him; and he vanished out of their sight."

* The appearance of the risen Christ at Emmaus and Jerusalem is told in Luke 24:13-49.

The startled men called for Jesus, but he was gone. They did not try to find him outdoors, but hurried back to Jerusalem to the hiding place of the eleven disciples. At that moment Jesus appeared again, frightening the disciples, who thought he was a ghost.

Luke's story struggles with a reality which cannot be touched and handled, proved or demonstrated in the usual way. It is the reality of faith. According to the last part of Luke's Gospel:

He was known to them in the breaking of bread.

He was not a spirit from the dead.

He opened their minds to understand the Scriptures.

He commissioned them to be witnesses.

He promised power from on high.

Luke set down this testimony of the early church some forty or more years after the Resurrection. In all those years Christians had learned that all five of the testimonies of Luke's Gospel were true because Christ is indeed risen from the dead.

64. Doubt and Assurance in the Upper Room*

It was the third day after the horror of the Crucifixion. Singly and by twos and by roundabout ways through Jerusalem, the disciples made their way to the secret room. No one could get into that room without giving an unmistakable sign that he was not an enemy. The men inside were afraid of another Judas, another traitor. They feared that someone might come, leading an armed band to arrest the followers of the man who had been executed as a political criminal.

Each time a man was admitted to the room, the door was shut again. The closed door was a sign of fear and uncertainty. Never

---

* John 20:19-31 is the source for stories of Jesus' appearance in the closed room in Jerusalem.

before had it been necessary for the disciples to be cooped up like chickens at night. Jesus and his disciples had always moved about freely. They had never before hidden themselves in a house.

That evening ten men saw that closed room turn to a place of joy like the joy of heaven. Suddenly Jesus was there. He was no longer a man like themselves, but the heavenly Christ.

Yet he was also the same Jesus they had always known. The spike marks on his hands and feet were unmistakable.

Jesus bestowed upon them a benediction of peace. It was the peace of the Blessed One of God.

Jesus gave the disciples his work to do—to forgive sins and to "retain" them. Then, as suddenly as he had come, he was gone.

There was no sleep that night as the disciples talked over the strange and startling experience. Many words of Scripture took on new meaning. The men remembered many things Jesus had said which they had not been able to understand before.

Later on, as the Gospel of John tells the story, the ten disciples tried to explain to the missing man, Thomas, what had happened. They went over the experience in as much detail as they could. It was difficult to tell someone about something which can only be known directly and personally.

"Maybe you did have a vision," Thomas admitted. "But I have no vision."

The more the disciples argued, the more stubborn Thomas became. "I can only believe what I touch and see myself," he declared. "If the Master is alive, let him show himself to me! Then I will decide whether it is true or not." Thomas was a hardheaded realist.

A week later, all the prudent, sensible, matter-of-fact ideas of Thomas were swept away like a pile of fallen leaves in the autumn wind. In the same Upper Room, along with the other ten disciples, Thomas saw and knew and worshiped. What had happened before, happened again: Jesus was suddenly there with the disciples.

"My Lord and my God!" was all that the doubting disciple could say, and he said it on his knees. Thomas was as over-whelmed as Isaiah had been in the Temple long ago when he saw the Lord, high and lifted up.

Every doubt was swept away—not because Thomas or Peter or Nathanael or any of the other disciples wanted to believe, but because they could not do anything but believe. They did not work their way into the presence of the risen Christ. Instead, he came to them and invited them into a new world of joy and hope.

What questions the men must have asked!

"When will the kingdom come?" James and John may have asked.

"What does it mean for a man to come back from the dead?" asked a thoughtful disciple.

"What does God mean with this mighty act?" asked one who remembered other mighty acts of God in Scripture.

If such were the questions of the disciples, the Gospel of John has nothing to say about them. It does not explain. It only testifies to the astonishing fact of the Resurrection as a fact of faith:

> *Blessed are those who have not seen*
> *and yet believe.*

65. A Catch of Exactly 153 Fish*

"Go to Galilee!" That was what the women had heard in the vision at the empty tomb. The gospel story testifies to times Jesus appeared in Jerusalem, the city where he had spent the last week of his earthly life. The story also testifies to times Jesus appeared in his homeland in Galilee.

The disciples had gone back to their trade as fishermen. Of the eleven men, seven stayed together. They were back on the familiar shore of the Sea of Galilee. Once Peter had thought he had given up fishing forever. Now he was again the leader of a band of

Blessed are those who have not seen
  and yet believe.

fishermen. The men sailed out in the night and let down their nets in places where they used to pull in the fish. But they caught nothing.

Early in the misty dawn, as the boat drew near the shore, the disciples saw a man standing on the beach. They did not recognize him. The man told them to try once more on the right side of the boat. Again they let their nets slide into the water. Suddenly the ropes tightened. The boat listed to one side with the pull of the net. Filled with fish, the net was too heavy to pull up into the boat.

The man on the beach did not go away. Suddenly the disciples recognized that this was Jesus. This time he was with them in the midst of their daily work.

When the disciples reached the shore, they found a fire burning and fish broiling over the charcoal. Bread had been laid out for breakfast. Silent and awestricken, the men joined in the meal to which Jesus invited them. But they dared not ask him any questions.

Like good fishermen they had beached the catch of fish first and stored it in baskets. A count tallied exactly 153 fish, and the load had not torn the net!

Not even Peter dared to speak to Jesus, for his heart was still burdened by his threefold denial of his Master. That burden was lifted from Peter's heart in a wonderful way. Jesus turned to Peter and spoke to him personally. Three times he asked a question and each time the question became more solemn. "Simon, son of John, do you love me more than these?"

---

* The story of Jesus' appearance at the Sea of Galilee is told in John 21. Did the number 153 have a hidden meaning? Some suppose that it had a symbolic meaning because in ancient times it was believed there were just 153 kinds of fish. The number may have been used as a symbol of all peoples. If that is the case, John's Gospel hints that all nations and races of mankind will be gathered in the net of the kingdom at the command of the risen Christ.

Once Peter had assured Jesus that though all others might forsake him, he, Peter, would never do so.

Now Peter blushed. He was no longer boastful, but he knew in his heart that there was no one else in all the world whom he could love the way he loved Jesus. "You know," he said quietly.

And three times Jesus assured Peter. Though Peter had forsaken his Lord, Jesus had never forsaken him. Now Jesus commissioned Peter to be an apostle.

"Tend my sheep," said Jesus, the Good Shepherd.

The Resurrection meant that the work which God had begun in Jesus would go on. It would go on through the disciples. Wherever the GOOD NEWS spread, Jesus, the Christ, would be present in the Spirit.

66. "Ascended into Heaven"*

He "ascended into heaven" is a statement of Christian faith. "Ascended" does not mean that Jesus climbed up to that mysterious height or that he soared beyond our universe. Rather, it means that "he was taken up" by the power and glory of God. The ascension of Christ is as mysterious as his birth in our world.

Luke's Gospel takes us to a hilltop near Bethany. There, within sight of the city where he had been crucified and buried and in the company of his disciples, Jesus parted from them. This was a parting which did not lessen the joy which the disciples had. Raising his hand, Jesus gave the disciples his benediction. Then the One they could see and hear with their physical senses was taken from them. But he would continue to be present in the Spirit with all his disciples everywhere—in Jerusalem, in Samaria, in Judea, to the end of the world.

* Only the Gospel of Luke has an account of the Ascension, Luke 24: 50-53. See also Acts 1:9-11.

Luke's Gospel does not explain or try to answer our curious questions. It simply states, "This is what we believe as Christians." The GOOD NEWS in the gospel story has no ending. It opens out into the story of the church of Jesus Christ. Wherever Christians gather, the joy of the risen Christ is with them and will be with them for all eternity.